新谷尚紀
Takanori Shintani 監修

Andrew P.Bourdelais 英文監訳

伝えたい "ニッポンの心"！
英語対訳で読む日本のしきたり

JIPPI
Compact

実業之日本社

装幀●杉本欣右
イラスト●笹森　識
日本文執筆●中村英良＋森井美紀
英文執筆●中堂良紀
DTP・編集●スタジオスパーク

　日本人なら誰でも子供の頃から親しみ、ごく当たり前のことと考えている「日本のしきたり」ですが、外国人の目から見ると、その多くが不思議なものとして映るようです。

　本書は、日本人として改めて「日本のしきたり」を見直すことができ、外国人の皆さんにも正しく理解していただけるよう、英語対訳で紹介する「日本のしきたり」の入門書です。

　「しきたり」は、歴史の流れの中で培われてきたものであり、その由来や発生の過程が不明確なものも数多く見受けられます。また、研究者の見解の相違から、書籍などでも記述が異なっている場合があります。

　本書では、内容の信頼性を高めるため、民俗学の研究者で「日本のしきたり」に精通した新谷尚紀先生のご指導をいただきました。ただし、英語対訳の入門書という本書の性格上、文字数にも限りがあり、概略の解説にとどまっている項目もあります。さらに詳しくお知りになりたい方は、巻末に紹介した参考図書をご参照いただければと思います。

　英訳につきましては、中学生レベルの英語力で理解できること、また英語を母国語とする人々が自然に読めることの二つを目標に、中堂良紀氏、アンドリュー　P.　ボーダレー氏にご尽力いだたきました。

　日本固有のものや儀式を表わす言葉を英訳するのは、大変困難な作業です。たとえば、「しめ縄」の英訳については、最後まで意見が分かれたところです。多くの英和辞典には「straw festoon」とありますが、「しめ縄」が神聖な場所を示すというニュアンスを強調して、本書では「holy rope」としました。このように、本書では辞書にある訳語をそのまま使うのではなく、「中学生レベルの英語力で理解できる」という意図に沿って訳出してあります。したがって、本書の訳語は必ずしも学術的に正確ではない場合がある、という点をご理解いただければ幸いです。

　本書が読者の皆さんの英語力向上の一助となり、また、外国からのお客さまとの正しいコミュニケーションのきっかけとしてご活用いただければ、これに過ぎる喜びはありません。

Most Japanese traditions, which are familiar to Japanese people, even to small children, sometimes seem mysterious to foreign people.

This book is an introduction to Japanese traditions. It was written for Japanese people to brush up on their traditions, as well as, to help non-Japanese people understand them better.

Many traditions have originated a long time ago and changed over the years so we don't know where many of them come from or why they were started. Many scholars have written differing opinions in their books.

This book was written under the supervision of a researcher of ethno-folklorist of Japan Prof. Shintani Takanori, who is a specialist in Japanese traditions.

Therefore the information is highly reliable. However, this book is a guide book for beginners and we were only able to give brief outlines about some traditions because of space limitations. For details, read the reference books at the end of this book.

Mr. Andrew P. Bourdelais and Mr. Nakado Yoshiki worked hard on translating the Japanese into simple English so that Japanese readers, who studied English in junior high school and native English speakers, will be able to enjoy reading it. It was very hard to translate ideas and ceremonies specific to Japan into English. For example, we discussed the matter of the translation for *shime-nawa* for a long time. Although we found the translation, "straw festoon" in many Japanese-English dictionaries, we decided to use "holy rope" to stress that it symbolizes a holy place. For this reason, we sometimes chose not to use translations from dictionaries. Instead, we used simple words so that Japanese readers with junior-high-school-level-English would enjoy reading it. Please understand that there are some instances where simplified versions of more scholarly correct words were used in this book.

We hope that this book will help you improve your English, as well as, provide opportunities to communicate with English speakers about Japanese traditions.

Chapter 1

....

Traditoins of Each Season / 季節のしきたり 9

Traditions for Lifetime Events / 人生のしきたり 　　　*61*

Chapter 3

....

Traditions in Daily Life / 暮らしのしきたり *113*

Chapter 4

Traditions of Each Season

第 1 章

季節のしきたり

1. The New Year

①Japan has four different seasons and has many traditions
<u>しきたり</u>
for <u>each</u> season. ②The Japanese people think the most
<u>それぞれの</u>
important tradition is in <u>the New Year's</u>.
<u>正月</u>
③January 1 is called *Gan-jitsu*. ④It is believed that this day

was to <u>welcome</u> the *Toshigami-sama* god, the Year god,
<u>〜をもてなす</u>
who visits people's houses on <u>New Year's Eve</u>. ⑤People
<u>大晦日</u>
thought that the *Toshigami-sama* god <u>made people one year</u>
<u>〜に1歳年をとらせる</u>
<u>older</u> and <u>brought happiness</u> to them. ⑥They also thought
<u>〜に幸福をもたらした</u>
that <u>the harvest of the year</u> and their happiness <u>depended</u>
<u>その年の収穫</u>   <u>〜に依存した</u>
<u>on</u> the god.

⑦Therefore, <u>New Year's Day</u> <u>spent with</u> the god <u>was</u>
<u>元日</u>   <u>〜と過ごした</u>
<u>thought to be</u> <u>the holiest day</u> of the year and people made
<u>〜であると考えられた</u> <u>もっとも神聖な日</u>
many rules to welcome the god.

⑧In Japan, <u>companies</u> and schools are closed at <u>the end of</u>
<u>会社</u>   <u>年末</u>
<u>the year</u> and people <u>get ready</u> to welcome the god. ⑨They
<u>〜する準備をする</u>
clean their houses, and <u>put out</u> *kado-matsu*, <u>gate pines</u>, and
<u>〜を飾る</u>   <u>門の松</u>

shime-nawa, a holy rope decoration, which are customs
神聖な縄の飾り　　　　　　　　　　　　　　　　　人々が始めた習慣

<u>people started</u> to welcome the god. ⑩*Kagami-mochi*, a

mirror-shaped rice cake, is made as <u>an offering</u> to the god.
鏡の形をした　　　　　　　　　　　　　　　　　供物

⑪<u>As time goes by</u>, people <u>tend to forget</u> the *Toshigami-*
時が過ぎ行くにつれて　　　　　　　　　　　〜を忘れがちである

sama god but the customs of people cleaning their houses at

the end of the year <u>is still followed</u> in many families today.
今でも行なわれている

---

1. 正月

①四季の変化がはっきりとしている日本には、季節ごとにさまざまなしきたりがあります。②その中で一番大切にされているのが**正月**です。

③1月1日は元日（がんじつ）と呼ばれます。④大晦日（おおみそか）に家々を訪れる年神（としがみ）さまをもてなす日と考えられてきました。⑤年神さまは、人々に年齢と新しい年の幸福をもたらすと信じられていました。⑥この神さまによってその年の収穫や人々の幸せが左右されると考えられていたのです。

⑦そのため、年神さまと過ごす元日は1年のうちでもっとも神聖な日と考えられ、神さまをお迎えするための、さまざまなしきたりが生まれました。

⑧日本の会社や学校は年末から休みになり、人々は年末に神さまを迎える準備をします。⑨家の中をきれいに掃除（そうじ）して、「**門松**（かどまつ）」や「**しめ縄**（なわ）」を飾りますが、これらは神さまを迎える準備として始められた習慣です。⑩そして、神さまへの供物（くもつ）として「**鏡餅**（かがみもち）」をお供（そな）えします。

⑪時代の流れとともに年神さまのことは忘れられつつありますが、年末に大掃除をする習慣は、今でも多くの家庭に残っています。

2. The First Visit of the Year to Shrines or Temples

①In the old days, people did the *toshi-gomori* custom, where
昔には
they stayed at home from New Year's Eve to the morning of
大晦日
New Year's Day and stayed up all night to pray for the
寝ないでいる   ～が来るのを祈る
coming of the *Toshigami-sama* god. ②This *toshi-gomori*

custom changed to making the visit on New Year's Eve and
～に変わった 除夜詣
making another visit on the morning of New Year's Day.
元旦詣
③In the late *Edo* period, it became popular among
江戸時代後期に
townspeople and others to visit shrines located in the lucky
町方
direction of the year, called *e-ho-mairi*. ④*E-ho* means the

direction in which the *Toshigami-sama* god is in and it is
～がいる方向
decided by the Chinese zodiac sign of the year.
えと
⑤In the *Meiji* period, the government led people to carry
明治時代に   ～を行なう
out the religious service of *Shinto* under the government
祭祀   国家政策として
policy. ⑥Therefore, people were encouraged to visit
奨励された
Ujigami-sama, the protecting gods, or *chinju-no-yasiro*,
守る神(→氏神)
village shrines, dedicated in their village or town, so that
鎮守の社 ～に祀られた

these visits soon became popular. ⑦At that time, some

railroads were built for visitors to take to shrines, like the
　　　　　　　　　　　　　参拝客が〜へ乗って行くように

Narita railroad (JR *Narita* Line). ⑧*E-ho* lost its meaning
成田鉄道　　　　　　　　　　　　　意味を失った

partly because those railroads began announcing yearly as
〜という理由もあって　　　　　　　毎年〜かのように宣伝すること

if the shrines along their lines were in the lucky direction

of the year.

---

2. 初詣

①古くは、大晦日（おおみそか）から元旦（がんたん）にかけて神社や家にこもり、寝ないで年神（としがみ）さまが来るのを祈願する「**年ごもり**」が行なわれていました。②この年ごもりが、大晦日の夜にお参りする「**除夜詣**（じょやもうで）」と元日の朝の「**元旦詣**（がんたんもうで）」になりました。

③江戸時代後期には、「恵方」（えほう）と呼ばれる方向にある神社にお参りする「恵方参り」が、江戸の町方などのあいだで盛んになりました。④恵方というのは年神さまがいる方向で、その年の「えと」によって決まります。

⑤明治時代になると、国家神道（しんとう）として、国が率先して神社の祭祀（さいし）を行なうようになりました。⑥そのため、村や町に祀（まつ）られていた氏神（うじがみ）や鎮守（ちんじゅ）の社（やしろ）への**初詣**（はつもうで）が推奨されて、盛んになりました。⑦おりしも普及し始めた鉄道の中には、成田鉄道（現在のJR成田線）のように神社への参拝客を見越して敷設（ふせつ）されたものもあります。⑧それらが毎年、沿線の神社が恵方であるかのような宣伝をしたこともあって、恵方の意味は失われました。

3. The Gate Pine and the Holy Rope Decoration

①The *Kado-matsu*, gate pine, is decoration made of pine
飾り物
tree branches and bamboo. ②It is put up outside both sides
松の木の枝　　　　竹　　　　　　～の外に設置される　　玄関の左右
of the front door during the New Year.

③Ancient people thought that gods were in pine trees. ④In
神
the old days, people put out only pine tree branches, and
昔に
bamboo was added to the decoration long after that.
～に組み合わされた　　　　　　そのずっとあとに
⑤Bamboo, which grows straight, is the symbol of human
まっすぐに成長する　　象徴　　　　人間の成長
growth. ⑥By adding bamboo to the pine tree, which is the
symbol of long life, the decoration became what the *kado-*
長生き　　　　　　　　　　現在の～
matsu is today.

⑦*Shime-kazari*, a holy rope decoration, is also used to
welcome the god. ⑧It is said that it comes from a Japanese
～を歓迎する　　　　～といわれている　　～に由来する　日本の神話
myth. ⑨*Amaterasu-omikami*, the goddess of the sun, hid in
～に隠れた
Ama-no-iwato cave and the whole world got dark.
天岩戸　　　　　　　　　　　　　　　　　　　暗くなった
⑩After she was taken out of the cave and the world became
～から連れ出された　ほら穴　　　　　　　明るくなった
bright, other gods blocked the cave with rope so that
～で―を閉ざした　　　　　　　～が―できないように

14

Amaterasu-omikami couldn't hide again. ⑪Because of this
　　　　　　　　　　　　　　　　　　　　　　　～によって
myth, rope has come to be used as the mark of holy places.
　　　　　　　　　　　　　　　　～の目印として　　　神聖な場所
⑫*Shime-kazari* differs from one area to another, but a
　　　　　　　　　異なる　　　　　　　　　地域によって
typical one is made with daphniphyllum, Japanese bitter
典型的な　　　　　　　　　ダフニフィルム　　　ゆずり葉
orange, and sorbus japonica. (see p.23)
橙　　　　　　ソルブス　ジャポニカ
　　　　　　　　裏白

---

3. 門松としめ飾り

①門松というのは、松と竹を組み合わせた飾り物です。②正月
にはこれを玄関の左右に飾ります。

③松の木は、神さまが宿る木とされていました。④これはその
昔、玄関に飾ったのが始まりで、竹と組み合わせるようになっ
たのは、ずっとあとになってからです。

⑤まっすぐに伸びる竹は、人間の成長を象徴しています。⑥こ
れを人間の長寿を象徴する松に添えることによって、現在のよ
うな形の門松になりました。

⑦しめ飾りも神さまを迎えるためのものです。⑧その由来とさ
れる日本神話もあります。⑨太陽の神である天照大神が天岩
戸に隠れ、世の中は闇になってしまいました。⑩そこから神を
出させて光明が戻ったとき、再び隠れないようにと、神々が
岩戸の入り口に縄を張りました。⑪この神話から、縄は神聖な
場所を示す目印として使われるようになりました。

⑫しめ飾りは地域によって違いがありますが、その代表的なも
のには、ゆずり葉、橙、裏白があしらわれています。

4. New Year's Food

①The food people eat for New Year's is called *osechi* food.
正月　　　　　　　　　　　　　　　　　〜と呼ばれる　おせち料理

②On the Japanese calendar, there are special days called
日本の暦

sekku, when a season changes to another, and *osechi* food
季節が変わる

was originally eaten on those days. ③The words "*osechi*
もともと

food" have come to be used for the food we eat for New
〜のために使われるようになった

Year's, one of the *sekku*.

④Traditional *osechi* food is put in lacquered four square
　　　　　　　　　　　　　　　　〜に入れられる　漆器の

stacking food boxes. ⑤Food eaten with *sake* is put in the
4重の四角い食べ物を入れる箱　酒と食べられる食べ物

top box. ⑥Grilled seafood, such as yellowtail and squid is
一番上の段　魚介の焼き物　　　　　　　ブリ　　　　　イカ

put　in the second box. ⑦Boiled food is put in the third
煮物

box, and food dressed with vinegar, including red-and-
　　　酢でドレッシングされた食べ物(→酢の物)　〜を含む

white vegetables, is put in the bottom box.
野菜

⑧The food put in the boxes has special meanings. ⑨For

example, *tatsukuri*, which is dried sardines with melted
　　　　　　　　　　　　　　　乾燥したイワシ　　　溶かした砂糖

sugar, means "making rice fields" and is the symbol of
　　　　　　　　　　　　　　　　　　　　　　　象徴

good crops. ⑩Some of the special meanings are in the color
豊作　　　　　　　　　　　　　　　　　　　　色や形に

and shape of the food. ⑪*Sudako* and *kamaboko* have beautiful red and white colors which the Japanese people believe are special. ⑫Rolled foods, such as *datemaki* and

巻物

kobumaki, have a shape similar to rolled books in the old

~と似た形　　　　昔の巻いた本

days, and symbolize the development of culture. (see p.22)

文化の発展

---

4. おせち料理

①正月に食べる料理は、**おせち料理**と呼ばれています。②日本の暦では季節の変わり目に節句という特別な日がありますが、おせち料理というのは、もともと節句に食べる料理という意味でした。③これが、やがて節句の一つである元旦に食べる料理を指すようになったのです。

④正式なおせち料理は、漆器の正方形の容器を４段重ねにした、**重箱**に盛りつけます。⑤一番上の段は、酒の肴を盛りつけます。⑥２段目にはブリ、イカなどの海の幸の焼き物を詰めます。⑦３段目は煮物を、一番下の段は紅白なますなどの酢の物を詰めます。⑧盛りつけられる料理には、それぞれ意味があります。⑨たとえば、カタクチイワシを乾燥したものに溶かした砂糖を絡めてつくる「田つくり」は、田んぼをつくることを意味し、豊作の象徴です。⑩そのほか、色や形が特別な意味を表す料理もあります。⑪酢ダコやカマボコは、日本でめでたいとされている紅白の彩を添えます。⑫また、伊達巻や昆布巻のような巻物は、形が昔の書物に似ているため、文化の繁栄を意味した料理です。

5. New Year's Ceremonial Sake

① One important Japanese tradition is that all family
大切な日本のしきたり

members drink *o-toso*, New Year's ceremonial *sake*,
儀式的な

together on the morning of January 1. ② *O-toso* is made by

putting *toso-san*, a mixture of herbs such as Japanese
~に入れること　　　　　~を混ぜたもの　薬草　　　　山椒

pepper and parsnip, in *sake* or in the sweet *sake* usually
防風　　　　　　　　　　　　　　　　　みりん

used for cooking. ③ In the old days, the Chinese people
昔には

drank it for their youth and long life, and it was introduced
不老長寿　　　　　　　　　　　　　~に紹介された

into Japan during the *Heian* period. ④ It came to be used in
平安時代

the New Year's ceremony at court and later became popular
元旦の儀式　　　　　　　宮中での~

among the general public.
庶民

⑤ Today, in general, all family members drink it together on
一般的に

the morning of January 1. ⑥ Traditionally, you drink *o-toso* in
伝統的には　　　　~を飲み干す

a cup with three sips, and pass the cup to the person next to
3口で　　　　　　　　　　　~を一に渡す

you. ⑦ The youngest person would drink first, and the others
最年少者　　　　　　　　　　　　　　　　その他の人

in order of age, but from the *Meiji* period, it became the
年齢順に　　　　　　　　明治時代　　　　　　　習慣

custom for the father, the head of the family, to drink first.
家長

⑧Traditionally, they use a *toso-ki* set, which is made up of
屠蘇器　　　　　　　　　　　　～から構成される

three cups on top of another, a small kettle-shaped container
3つ重ねの盃　　　　　　　　　　　やかんの形をした容器(→銚子)

and a *sake* stand. ⑨It is a tradition that they fill the cup using
盃台　　　　　　　～という伝統がある

the *sake* container in three pours. ⑩The ceremony of sitting
3回(注ぎ)で　　　　　　～する儀式

around the *toso-ki* set and saying, "Happy New Year!" was a

typical sight at New Year's in Japan. (see p.22)
典型的な光景

---

5. お屠蘇

①1月1日の元日の朝、家族そろって**お屠蘇**を飲むのも、日本の正月の大切なしきたりの一つです。②お屠蘇というのは、山椒や防風などの薬草を混ぜた「屠蘇散」を、日本酒やみりんに浸してつくります。③もともと中国で不老長寿の薬酒として飲まれていたものが平安時代に日本に伝わりました。④それが宮中の元旦の儀式に使われるようになり、やがて庶民の間に広まりました。

⑤現在は、元日の朝に家族全員で飲むのが一般的です。⑥正式には盃に注がれたお屠蘇を3口で飲み干し、次の人に盃を回します。⑦若い人から飲むのが正式とされていますが、明治以降、家長である父親から飲む習慣も生まれました。

⑧本来、お屠蘇には3つ重ねの盃と銚子、盃台がセットになった**屠蘇器**が使われます。⑨銚子から盃に、3回に分けて注ぐのが正式とされています。⑩元日の朝、家族で屠蘇器を囲み、新年の挨拶をする光景は、日本の正月を象徴するものでした。

6. New Year's Allowance and New Year's Gift

①It is an old custom in Japan for older people to give an
allowance to younger people for New Year's. ②This custom
of New Year's allowance spreaded widely a long time ago,
and a lot of people follow it, but at that time, what they gave
was round rice cakes and not money. ③It is said that this
custom started when people gave round rice cakes to others
after offering them to the gods.④Because the gods were
said to be in these offerings, people thought they became
one year older and would have good health for the year by
eating the offerings.
⑤Although almost all the children in Japan get a New Year's
allowance today, it was only after the World War II that
many children started getting money as they do today.
⑥New Year's allowance is what people give to those below
them, but on the other hand, what people give to those
above them is called a New Year's gift. ⑦From January 2

to 7, not on January 1, people visit those above them, greet
　　　　　　　　　　　　　　　　　　　　　　　挨拶する
them and give them a New Year's gift. ⑧In the past, it was
　　　　　　　　　　　　　　　　　　　　以前
normal that New Year's calls were made, for example,
~はふつうのことだった　年始まわり
going to their clients to give towels, or visiting their
　　　　　　　得意先　　　　　　　タオル
relatives or bosses with a box of cakes. ⑨These days,
親戚　　　　上司　　　　　　菓子折り
however, this custom is also dying out .
　　　　　　　　　　　　　　なくなりつつある

---

6. 年玉と年賀

①正月に年長者が年少者に小遣いをあげる習慣があります。
②この**年玉**の習慣は古くから広く行なわれてきましたが、もと
もと年玉はお金ではなく、丸い餅でした。③これを神さまにお
供えしたあとで、配ったことから年玉の習慣が始まったとされ
ています。④神さまにお供えしたものには霊が宿るとされ、こ
れをいただくことによって一つ年をとり、その年も健康に過ご
せると考えられていたのです。

⑤現在のように、ほとんどの子どもたちがお金をもらえるよう
になったのは、戦後のことです。

⑥年玉は、目上の者が目下の者に贈るものですが、反対に目下
の者から目上の者に贈り物をするのが**年賀**です。⑦1月1日の
元日を避けて1月2日から7日までの間に訪問し、新年の挨拶
とともに年賀を贈ります。⑧得意先をまわってタオルを配った
り、菓子折りを持って親戚や上司を訪ねるといった年始まわ
りが、以前はごく一般的に行なわれていました。⑨しかし、最
近はこの習慣も薄れつつあります。

お節料理とお屠蘇

New Year's Food and Ceremonial Sake Set

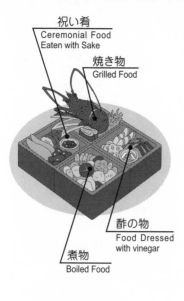

祝い肴
Ceremonial Food
Eaten with Sake

焼き物
Grilled Food

酢の物
Food Dressed
with vinegar

煮物
Boiled Food

元日には、家族そろって食卓を囲み、お屠蘇で新年を祝い、お節料理を食べます。

On January 1, all the family members sit around the table to celebrate the New Year drinking New Year's ceremonial *sake* and eating New Year's food.

屠蘇器
Ceremonial Sake Set

獅子舞

Lion Dance

木などでつくられた獅子の頭をかぶって踊る舞。正月や祭りなど縁起のいい日に行なわれます。

Danced by a performer wearing a lion's mask made from wood or other materials. This dance is performed on lucky days such as New Year's and other festival days.

しめ飾り
The Holy Rope Decoration

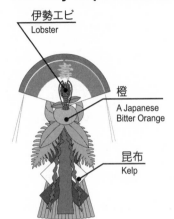

伊勢エビ
Lobster

橙
A Japanese
Bitter Orange

昆布
Kelp

年神さまをお迎えするための、神聖な場所を示す飾り物です。

This decoration marks a holy place used to welcome the Year god.

門松
The Gate Pine

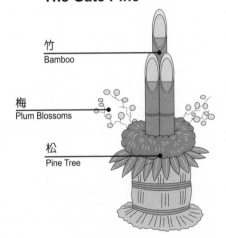

竹
Bamboo

梅
Plum Blossoms

松
Pine Tree

正月には、神さまが宿る木とされた松と、成長の象徴である竹を組み合わせた門松を、玄関に飾ります。

The gate pine decoration is placed outside the front door during the New Year. It is made from pine tree, which people believe the god is in, and bamboo, the symbol of human growth.

7. The Changing of Seasons

①Originally, *setsubun* meant the day one season turned to
もともと　　　　　　　　　　　　季節が変わる日

another, and there were four *setsubun* in a year. ②The day which

we call *setubun* today, February 3 (4 in some years), is the one

when winter turns to spring. ③It is the day before *risshun*, the
冬から春に変わる日

day on which spring begins according to the calendar.
　　　　　　　　　　　　　　　　　暦によると

④In the old days, people thought that devils came at the
昔には　　　　　　　　　　　　　　　　　　　　鬼

changing of seasons to bring disasters and make people
季節の変わり目に　　　　　　　　　　災い

sick. ⑤Bean throwing, or *mame-maki* is a custom to get the
　　　　　　　　　　　　　　　　　　　　　習慣

devils out of their house and bring in good luck. ⑥This
~を—から追い出す　　　　　　　　呼び込む　福

custom comes from an old Chinese ceremony, which was
　~に由来する　　　　　　　　　　儀式

introduced to Japan in the *Nara* period. ⑦Some people say
~に伝えられた　　　　奈良時代　　　　　~と言う人もいる

that *mame* is used because it sounds like *ma-metsu,* the
　　　　　　　　　　　　　　　~のように聞こえる

Japanese word which means beating the devil.
　　　　　　　　　　　　　~をやっつけること

⑧Men with the same zodiac sign as that year or men who
その年と同じえとを持つ男性(→年男)

are in the *yaku-doshi*, which is considered an unlucky year,
　　　　　　　　　　　　　不幸の歳だと考えられる年

throw the beans. ⑨When there is not such a person in the

family, the head of the household throws them. ⑩After
　　　　　一家の主人

opening all the windows and the front door, they throw
　　　　　　　　　　　　　　　　　　　　　　　　　　　投げる

beans out of the house saying, "Devils out!" and into the
　　　　～から外へ　　　～と言いながら　「鬼は外」　　　　～のうちへ

house saying, "Good luck in!". ⑪When they are finished,
　　　　　「福は内」

all the family members eat the same numbet of beans as
　　　　　　　　　　　自分の年齢と同じ数の豆

their age and pray for a safe new year. (see p.42)
　　　　　　　～を祈る

7. 節分

①もともとは、「節分」とは季節の変わり目を表す言葉であり、年4回の節分がありました。②現在の節分である2月3日（年によっては4日）は、その中で冬から春に変わる日を指します。③それは、暦の上で春が始まる「立春」の前日です。

④古くは、季節の変わり目に鬼がやってきて災いや疫病をもたらすと考えられていました。⑤家からこの鬼を追い出して福を招き入れるための風習が「豆まき」です。⑥その起源は中国に古くから伝わる儀式で、奈良時代に日本に伝わりました。

⑦一説によれば、豆が使われるのは、「魔滅」に通じ、魔を退治するという意味があるからです。

⑧豆をまくのは年男と呼ばれるその年がえとの男性、あるいはその年に厄年を迎える男性です。⑨もしもどちらもいない場合には、一家の主人がまきます。⑩家の窓や玄関をすべて開け放ち、「鬼は外」と叫びながら外に向かってまき、次に「福は内」と叫びながら中に向かってまきます。⑪豆まきが終わると、家族全員がそろって、それぞれの年の数だけ豆を食べ、その年の無事を祈ります。

8. The Doll Festival

①March 3 is called the Peach *sekku*, or the Doll Festival,
桃の節句　　　　　　　　　　　　　雛祭り

when people pray for the healthy growth and happy future
健やかな成長

of girls. ②The first Peach *sekku* for a baby girl after birth is
女の赤ん坊

called the first *sekku*. ③It is a tradition that the family on
初節句　　　　　　～というしきたりがある　　母親の実家

the mother's side gives dolls to the baby girl and have a big

party for her. ④*Sekku* was originally the day one season
もともと　　季節の変わり目の日

turned to another according to the Chinese calendar. ⑤In
中国の暦

the *Edo* period, the five *sekku* – *jinjitsu* on January 1, *joshi*
江戸時代に　　　5節句

on March 3, *tango* on May 5, *shichiseki* on July 7, and

choyo on September 9 – became holidays. ⑥These five
祭日

days were not holidays any more in the *Meiji* period, but
もはや～ではなかった　　　　　　明治時代に

the traditions on those days are kept even today.
守られている

⑦In the *Heian* period, there was a custom of giving people's
平安時代に　　　　　　　　～する習慣があった

own uncleanness to paper dolls, or *hito-gata*, and floating
自分自身のけがれ　　　　　　　　　　　　　　　　　川に～を流すこと

them down the river on March 3. ⑧In the court, it became
宮廷で

popular among noble girls to play wirh dolls, which was
貴族の女子

26

called *hiina-asobi*.

⑨These two customs combined into a new custom where girls

slept with dolls by their pillow on the night of March 3, and

            枕元に

then the dolls were purified at temples or shrines the next

            お祓いをしてもらった

morning. ⑩This is the origin of the Doll Festival.(see p.42)

      起源

---

8. 雛祭り

①３月３日は「**桃の節句**」、「**雛祭り**」と呼ばれ、女の子の健やかな成長と将来の幸せを祈る日です。②特に女の子が生まれて初めて迎える桃の節句は「**初節句**」と呼ばれます。③母親の実家が孫に雛人形を贈り、盛大にお祝いするしきたりがあります。④節句は、もともとは中国の暦で定められた季節の変り目の日でした。⑤江戸時代になると、１月７日の人日、３月３日の上巳、５月５日の端午、７月７日の七夕、９月９日の重陽が５節句として祭日に定められました。⑥明治時代になって、５節句は祭日ではなくなりましたが、これらの日に行なわれたしきたりは現代にいたるまで伝えられています。

⑦平安時代には３月３日の上巳に、人形にけがれを移し、川に流す習慣がありました。⑧一方、平安時代の貴族の女の子の遊びとして、人形で遊ぶ「**雛遊び**」が流行しました。

⑨この二つが結びつき、雛人形を３月３日の夜に枕元に置いて眠り、翌朝に寺や神社でお祓いをしてもらう習慣が生まれました。⑩これが雛祭りの起源です。

9. The Equinoctial Week

①There are two days a year on which the length of daytime
（その日は）（日中の長さ）
is equal to that of nighttime. ②Japanese people call them
（〜と等しい）（夜の長さ）
shunbun-no-hi, or Spring Equinox Day and *shubun-no-hi,* or
（春の昼夜の長さが同じ日）
Autumnal Equinox Day . ③The seven days which start
（秋の昼夜の長さが同じ日）
three days before the equinox and end three days after are

called the equinoctial week, or *higan.*
（彼岸）

④*Higan* means the other shore, and this word comes from
（向こう岸(→彼岸)）（〜に由来する）
Buddhism. ⑤*Higan* is the world in which people are above
（仏教）（〜を超越した）
their illusions of themselves and desires and *higan* also
（迷い）（欲望）
means the other world. ⑥It was believed that the distance
（あの世）（〜だと信じられた）（〜と—の距離）
between this shore and the other shore was the shortest on

the equinox days, so that Buddhist ceremony called *higan-e*
（仏教儀式）
was held in temples to pray for the dead.
（〜を弔う）（死者）
⑦Recently, it is not common to take part in *higan-e.*
（〜するのは一般的ではない）（〜に参加する）
⑧However, many people do visit their ancestors' graves
（先祖の墓）
because they think this is the day to remember the dead,

like the Christian All Souls' Day.
　　　　　キリスト教の死者の日

⑨During the equinoctial week, Japanese people eat *bota-*

mochi, which is a rice ball covered with bean paste.
　　　　　　　　　　　　　豆の練りもので包んだご飯の玉

⑩Because the color red was thought to keep out evil spirits,
　　　　　　　　　　　　　　　　　　　　　　～を近寄せない　　邪気

it is said that people used to offer rice balls covered with red
～といわれている　　　　　　　　～を—にお供えする

bean paste to the dead and pray for them during this week.

---

9. 彼岸

①1年に2回、昼と夜の長さが同じになる日があります。②それらの日を**春分の日、秋分の日**と呼んでいます。③その前後3日を合わせた7日間が「**彼岸**」です。

④彼岸とは、向こう岸という意味で、もともとは仏教用語です。⑤迷いや欲望を超越した者の世界が彼岸であり、同時に死後の世界も意味します。⑥昼と夜の長さが同じになる日は、彼岸が一番近くなると信じられていたため、寺ではこの時期に死者を弔う「**彼岸会**」と呼ばれる仏教儀式が行なわれてきました。

⑦最近は、彼岸会に行くことはあまり一般的ではありません。⑧しかし、キリスト教の死者の日のように死者をしのぶ日とされ、多くの人々が墓参りに出かけます。

⑨彼岸に食べる料理に、「ぼた餅」というご飯を餡で包んだものがあります。⑩赤い色は邪気を払うと信じられていたことから、赤い餡で表面を包んだご飯を彼岸に死者に供え、供養するようになったといわれています。

10. Cherry Blossom Viewing

①*Hana-mi,* or cherry blossom viewing, is an event where people sit under blossoming cherry trees, drink *sake* and
満開の桜の木
enjoy the beauty of the blossoms. ②It is one of the most important seasonal events for the Japanese people. ③In
季節行事
spring, all the cherry trees in an area come into bloom at
ある地域において　　　開花する
once and then quickly fall from the tree after a short time.
いっせいに
④The short life of cherry blossoms, often compared to the
短い命　　　　　　　　　　　　　　　　　　　〜と比べられて
short life of humans, appeals to many Japanese people.
　　　　　　　　　　　　　　　　　　〜に訴えかける
⑤*Hana-mi* has become an important event, and it has much
　　　　　　　　　　　　　　　　　　　　　　　〜と大いに関係がある
to do with how Japanese view life, death and beauty.
　　　　　どのように日本人が〜を眺めるか
⑥*Hana-mi* is an old custom, and it is said that nobles in the
　　　　　　古い習慣　　　　　　　〜だといわれている　貴族
Nara period started it. ⑦At that time, people enjoyed plum
　　　　　　　　　　　　　　　　　　　　　　　　　　　梅の花
blossoms, but, in the *Heian* period, they began to enjoy
cherry blossoms. ⑧There was a plum tree on the left side of
　　　　　　　　　　　　　　　梅の木
the *Shishin-den* Palace's front, where the emperor lived, in
紫宸殿の正面　　　　　　　　　　　　　　　　　　　天皇
the *Heian* capital but it was replaced by a cherry tree after
平安京　　　　　　　〜に替えられた

it died.
枯れた

⑨Cherry Blossom Viewing was also an important event in

the rice farming villages, too. ⑩It was believed that the
稲作の農村

cherry blossoms told when the rice god would come and
いつ稲の神が来るか

the peasants forecasted how good their rice crop would be
農民　　　　　予想した　　稲の実りがどうなるか

that season by the condition of their blossoms.
様子

---

10. 花見

①「花見」は満開の桜の木の下で酒を飲みながら花を楽しむものです。②それは日本人にとって大切な季節行事の一つです。③桜は春の一時期に地域でいっせいに開花し短期間で散ってしまいます。④そのはかなさが、人の一生の短さにもたとえられ、日本人の心をとらえました。⑤これが春の大切な風物になり、死生観や美意識にも影響を与えています。

⑥花見を楽しむ習慣は古く、奈良時代の貴族が始めたといわれています。⑦その頃の花見は梅を観賞することでしたが、平安時代になると桜に変わりました。⑧天皇の住まいであった平安京紫宸殿の正面左には梅が植えられていましたが、枯れると桜に植え替えられました。

⑨一方、稲作をしている農村部でも、花見は重要な行事だったようです。⑩桜は稲の神の来訪を知らせる花と考えられており、桜の咲き具合で、稲の実りを占っていたようです。

11. The 88th Day

①*Hachiju-hachi-ya*, the 88th Day, is the day when spring
<u>春から夏へ変わる日</u>
turns to summer. ②When the Chinese characters for the
<u>漢字</u>
number eighty-eight (八十八) are rearranged, they get one
<u>並べかえられる</u>
character for "rice (米)". ③For this reason, this day has

been especially important for farmers.
<u>農民</u>
④*Hachiju-hachi-ya* is the eighty-eighth day from *risshun*,

when spring is thought to start. ⑤*Risshun* is in early
<u>春が始まると考えられる</u>
February of the solar calendar, so that the 88th day is
<u>新暦</u>
usually around May 2.

⑥Some farming areas of Japan have frost even in May.
<u>農業地帯</u> <u>霜</u>
⑦This frost often damaged crops so there used to be words
<u>傷めた</u> <u>農作物</u> <u>注意の言葉</u>
of caution, "late frost on the 88th day". ⑧Since there is little
<u>「八十八夜の忘れ霜」</u> <u>~する必要はほとんどない</u>
need to worry about frost after the 88th day, farmers began

to get ready for planting rice or paddy seeds then.
<u>~の準備をする</u> <u>種モミ</u>
⑨The first thing Japanese people today think of when they
<u>今日の日本人が最初に思い浮かべるもの</u>
hear "the 88th day" is the first tea of the year. ⑩Farmers
<u>新茶</u>

usually <u>pick</u> the first crop of tea around the 88th day
摘む
because the tea at that time <u>is filled with</u> <u>nutrients stored</u>
　　　　　　　　　　　　　　　〜でいっぱいの　蓄えられた養分
<u>over winter</u> and <u>most delicious</u>. ⑪<u>Tea picking</u> on the 88th
冬の間ずっと　　最もおいしい　　茶摘み
day <u>is sung about</u> in the song, "*Cha-tsumi*", which is famous
　　〜で歌われる
for the phrase, "The 88th day just before summer …."
　　　　　　　　　「夏も近づく八十八夜……」

---

11. 八十八夜

①<ruby>八十八夜<rt>はちじゅうはちや</rt></ruby>は、春から夏へ変わる日のことです。②「八十八」という漢数字を縦に並べると「米」という字になります。③そのことから、特に農業に<ruby>携<rt>たずさ</rt></ruby>わる人にとって大切な日とされてきました。

④八十八という数字は、春が始まる日とされている「<ruby>立春<rt>りっしゅん</rt></ruby>」から88日目であることを意味します。⑤新暦では立春は2月の上旬なので、八十八夜は5月の2日頃にあたります。

⑥日本の農村地帯では、5月になっても<ruby>霜<rt>しも</rt></ruby>が降ることがあります。⑦これが農作物に被害を与えるため、「八十八夜の忘れ霜」という、霜に対する注意を喚起する言葉もありました。⑧八十八夜を境に霜の心配もほぼなくなるため、昔の農民はこの日から<ruby>種<rt>たね</rt></ruby>モミをまいたり、田んぼで稲作をする準備にとりかかったのです。

⑨現代の日本人が八十八夜でまず思い浮かべるのは新茶です。⑩冬の間養分を<ruby>蓄<rt>たくわ</rt></ruby>えたチャノキの<ruby>新芽<rt>しんめ</rt></ruby>からつくる緑茶は味がいいことから、八十八夜の前後は茶の新芽を<ruby>摘<rt>つ</rt></ruby>む季節とされています。⑪「夏も近づく八十八夜……」で知られる「茶摘み」という歌にも、八十八夜に茶摘みをする風景が歌われています。

12. The Boy's Festival

①*Tango-no-sekku*, on May 5, is the day when people pray for
their boys to grow up healthy. ②In their houses, they put out
symbols of strength such as a special doll for boys and *samurai*
armor and a helmet in hope that their boys will grow up to be
strong. ③The special dolls can be of famous characters such as
Momotaro, a boy who defeats demons that do wrong to people
in a fairy tale, or of *Kintaro*, a boy who rides bear in a children's
song, or of old strong military generals. ④Outside the house,
people set up flying carp streamers, or *koi-nobori*. ⑤These carp
streamers comes from an ancient Chinese event that a carp
which swam up strong rapids became a dragon.
⑥*Tango-no-sekku* was originally a day for girls until the
samurai took over power and it was changed into a day for
boys. ⑦In May, farmers plant rice in their fields and it is called
ta-ue. ⑧Farmers believed that this planting was very important
and that young, innocent girls should do it. ⑨Therefore it was a

custom for those girls to stay in a hut to make their minds and
習慣　　　　　　　　　　　　　　　　　　　　　　　　　小屋

bodies pure on *tango-no-sekku*, just before planting. ⑩This hut

had a roof made from iris leaves with an herbal smell strong
　　〜でできた屋根　　菖蒲の葉

enough to keep away insects. ⑪Because the Japanese name for
　　　　〜を近づけない　虫たち

iris, *Shobu*, sounds like another Japanese word meaning "respect
　　　　　　　　　〜のように聞こえる

for the military", this day later became the Boy's Festival.
武芸を尊ぶこと

---

12. 端午の節句

①５月５日の「端午の節句」は男の子の無事な成長を祈る日です。
②この日には、男の子が丈夫に育つように、強さの象徴である５
月人形や鎧・兜を家に飾ります。③５月人形は、日本の童話の中
で人々を苦しめる鬼を退治する桃太郎や、童謡で熊にまたがった
とされている金太郎、昔の強い武将などを題材にしたものです。
④また、家の外には鯉のぼりを飾ります。⑤鯉のぼりは、急流を
登った鯉が龍になったという中国の故事に由来するものです。
⑥端午の節句が男の子の日になったのは、武士が台頭してからの
ことで、それ以前は女性の日でした。⑦５月になると、稲作農家
は田んぼに稲の苗を植える「田植え」をします。⑧これはとても
重要な作業であり、けがれを知らぬ若い女性の仕事とされていま
した。⑨そのために、田植えを控えた端午の節句に女性たちは小
屋にこもり、心身を清める習慣がありました。⑩小屋は、匂いが
強く、薬草のような虫除け効果がある菖蒲の葉でふかれていまし
た。⑪この「菖蒲」という音は「尚武（武を尊ぶ）」に通じるため、
後には男の子の節句となりました。

13. Seasonal Clothing Switch

①Since there is a big difference in the temperature between
〜のあいだの大きな気温差

summer and winter in Japan, people have to switch the type
服の種類を替える

of clothes they wear in each season. ②Students, police
警察官

officers, some office workers, and so on, have summer and
会社員　　　　　　　　　　　夏服と冬服

winter uniforms. ③The day on which one uniform is

switched for the other is called *koromo-gae*.

④Winter clothes are switched to summer clothes on June 1,

and summer clothes are switched back to winter clothes on

October 1. ⑤The history of switching clothes goes back to
〜にさかのぼる

the *Heian* period. ⑥In the court, at that time, April 1 and
平安時代　　　　　宮廷では

October 1 on the lunar calendar were called *ko-i*, which is

similar to switching of clothes today.
〜と似ている

⑦In the *Edo* period, the shogunate decided that *samurai*
江戸時代に　　　幕府　　　　　　　　　　　武士

should switch their clothes four times a year. ⑧This custom
習慣

became popular and took root among the general public,
根づいた　　　　庶民

too.

⑨June 1 and October 1 became the fixed days to switch
定められた日
clothes in the *Meiji* period. ⑩However, there are sometimes
明治時代に
many hot days in April and in October because of global
地球温暖化
warming. ⑪So even business men usually in a suit have
ふつうはスーツを着るサラリーマンでさえ
come to adjust their clothes according to weather and
〜を調整するようになってきた　　　〜にしたがって
temperature these days.

---

13. 衣替え

①日本は冬と夏で温度差が大きいために、冬と夏に服装を変え
なければなりません。②そのため、学生、警察官、特定の会社
員などの制服には必ず夏服と冬服が用意されています。③これ
を着替える日が「衣替え」です。

④現在は冬服から夏服に着替えるのが６月１日、夏服から冬服
に着替えるのが 10 月１日とされています。⑤衣替えの歴史は
平安時代までさかのぼることができます。⑥平安時代の宮中で
は、旧暦の４月１日と 10 月１日が「更衣」とされ、現在の衣
替えにあたる日でした。

⑦江戸時代は幕府が武士に対して、年４回の衣替えの日を定め
ていました。⑧これが庶民の間に広がり、定着しました。

⑨６月１日と 10 月１日が衣替えの日とされるようになったの
は、明治時代になってからのことです。⑩ただし、最近は地球
温暖化の影響によって４月や 10 月に暑い日が続くこともあり
ます。⑪そのため、スーツを着るサラリーマンなどは天候や気
温に合わせた服装を身に着けることが多くなってきました。

14. The Festival of Vega

①July 7 is *tanabata*, the Festival of Vega, one of the five
ベガ(織姫星)
important *sekku* in Japan which have the Peach Festival, the
桃の節句
Boy's Festival and so on. ②The true name of this day is
端午の節句
shichiseki but Japanese people usually call it *tanabata* in

Japanese. ③The *tanabata* festival comes from an old
～に由来する
Chinese legend about a cow handler and a weaver. ④The
古い中国の伝説   牛追い人   機織り人   織姫
weaver, Vega, was the daughter of Emperor *Ten-tei*, the
天帝
first god of Taoism. ⑤She fell in love with Altair, a cow
道教   ～と恋に落ちた   牽牛星
handler, and they got married. ⑥However, the two enjoyed
結婚した
their married life so much that they stopped working.
結婚生活
⑦Emperor *Ten-tei* got angry and separated them with the
天の川で引き離した
Milky Way. ⑧The only time they were able to meet after

that was on a clear night of *tanabata*. ⑨On that night, they
晴れた七夕の夜
could meet by using a bridge over the Milky Way made by

magpies. ⑩If it rained and the river rose, they could not
カササギ(鳥)   川が増水した
cross the bridge and see each other.
～を渡ることも―に会うこともできなかった

⑪Therefore, on the day before *tanabata*, people make *sasa-kazari* to pray for no rain on the night of *tanabata*.
～を祈るために

⑫*Sasa-kazari* is a bamboo branch with five different
竹の枝　　　　　　　　～に5色の短冊を結んだ

colored strips of paper tied to the leaves. ⑬People write

their wishes on these strips of paper. (see p.43)
願い事

---

14. 七夕

①7月7日は「桃の節句」や「端午の節句」と並ぶ5節句の一つである「**たなばた**」です。②漢字で「**七夕**」と書き、正しくは「しちせき」と読みますが、「たなばた」というのが一般的です。③七夕は、中国に古くから伝わる牽牛と織姫の伝説に由来するお祭りです。④機織りの織姫は道教の最高神である天帝の娘でした。⑤織姫は牛追いの牽牛と恋に落ち、結婚します。⑥ところが、二人は幸せな結婚生活を楽しむがあまりに働かなくなってしまいました。⑦怒った天帝は、天の川で二人の間を隔ててしまいます。⑧この二人が会えるのは、晴れた七夕の夜だけ。⑨カササギが天の川に橋をかけ、二人は会うことができるのです。⑩雨が降ると天の川の水量が増え、橋を渡れないので、二人は会うことができません。

　⑪そこで、人々は七夕の夜に雨が降らないことを祈りながら、前日に**笹飾り**をつくります。⑫笹飾りとは、笹の葉に5色の**短冊**をつるしたものです。⑬人々は短冊に願い事を書きます。

15. Midsummer Day of the Ox

① According to the Chinese doctrine of the five natural elements
~によると　中国の陰陽五行説

of positive and negative, everything can be represented by the
~で表すことができる

five elements of tree, fire, soil, metal and water. ② The seasons
土　金属

were divided into elements: spring is the tree, summer is fire,
~に分けられた

fall is metal, and winter is water. ③ Soil represents the changing
季節の変わり目

of seasons, and the last 18 days of each season were called *doyo*.

④ During this period, it was taboo to garden or bury the dead.
禁忌　　土いじりする　埋葬する

⑤ The Midsummer Day of the Ox is the day during *doyo* that is
土用丑の日

assigned the symbol of the ox according to the Chinese zodiac.
~が割り当てられた　丑の記号　　　　　　十二支

⑥ In the Chinese zodiac, each day and month are also assigned a

symbol just as each year is. ⑦ On the Midsummer Day of the
~とちょうど同じように

Ox, there is the custom, among the Japanese, of eating eel. ⑧ On
鰻

Midsummer Day of the Ox since the ancient times, legend had
古くから　　　　　　　～という言い伝えがあった

it that people wouldn't suffer from the summer heat if they ate
夏負けする

something that had a *hiragana* "u" in its name. ⑨ During that

time, an owner of an eel restaurant that wasn't doing well
店主　　　鰻屋　　　　　　繁盛していなかった

asked *Hiraga Gennai*, a Dutch scholar in the *Edo* period, for
　～に助言を求めた　　　　　　オランダの

advice. ⑩*Gennai* took advantage of the legend and put a sign up
　　　　　　　　　　～を利用した　　　　　　　　　　張り紙をした

at the restaurant telling people it was the Midsummer Day of

the Ox, and then many people came to eat eel or *unagi* in

Japanese. ⑪Some say that this is the start for the custom of

eating eel on Midsummer Day of the Ox today.

---

15. 土用の丑の日

①中国の陰陽五行説では、木、火、土、金、水の5つの元素で万物を表しています。②4つの季節は、「春を木」、「夏を火」、「秋を金」、「冬を水」に振り分けられました。③残った「土」は4つの季節の変わり目を表すものとし、各季節の終わりの18日間を土用としました。④この期間は土いじりや埋葬することは禁忌とされていました。

⑤土用の丑の日とは、土用のあいだで日の十二支が丑である日のこと。⑥年に十二支が割り振られているように、月も日も十二支が当てはまります。

⑦この土用の丑の日には、鰻を食べる習慣があります。⑧古くから、夏土用の丑の日に「う」のつくものを食べると、夏負けしないという言い伝えがありました。⑨江戸時代の蘭学者・平賀源内は、繁盛しなくて困っている鰻屋から相談を受けました。⑩その言い伝えを利用して店先に「本日、土用丑の日」と書いた紙を張りつけたところ、その店は大繁盛。⑪これがきっかけとなり、土用に鰻を食べる習慣が生まれたという伝説もあります。

節分の豆まき

Bean Throwing on the Day When Winter Turns to Spring

季節の変り目である節分に、豆を
まいて鬼に見立てた『厄』を追い
払います。

On this day, people throw beans
at a person wearing a devil's
mask in order to force all "bad
luck" out of their house.

雛祭りの雛人形

The Dolls of the Doll Festival

3月3日の雛祭りには、女の子の健やかな成長と将来の幸
せを祈って雛人形を飾ります。

For the Doll Festival on March 3, people put out dolls to
pray for the healthy growth and happy future of their
girls.

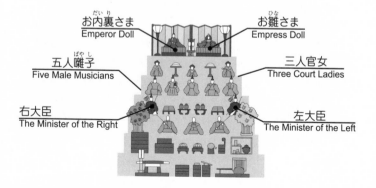

お内裏さま
Emperor Doll

お雛さま
Empress Doll

五人囃子
Five Male Musicians

三人官女
Three Court Ladies

右大臣
The Minister of the Right

左大臣
The Minister of the Left

端午の節句の鯉のぼりと鎧・兜

Flying Carp Streamers and Samurai Armor and Helmet for the Boy's Festival

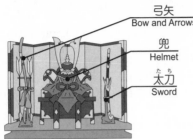

弓矢
Bow and Arrows

兜
Helmet

太刀
Sword

男の子が強く育つようにという願いを込めて、鎧・兜を飾ります。

People put out *samurai* armor and a helmet in hope that their boys will grow up to be strong.

急流を登った鯉が龍になったという中国の故事から、鯉は成長を意味します。

The Carp is a symbol of growth from an ancient Chinese event that a carp which swam up strong rapids became a dragon.

吹き流し
Streamer

真鯉
Black Carp

緋鯉
Red Carp

子鯉
Baby Carp

七夕の笹飾り

The Bamboo Decoration of the Festival of Vega

七夕には、願いごとを書いた短冊を笹竹につるします。

For the Festival of Vega, people write their wishes on strips of paper and tied them to the leaves of a bamboo branch.

16. The Bon Festival

①*O-bon*, or the *Bon* Festival, from July 13 to 15 on the
お盆　　　　　　　　　　　　　　　　　　　旧暦の
lunar calendar, is a seasonal event just as important for the
季節行事
Japanese as New Year's is. ②It is believed that the spirits of
正月　　　　　　　　～と信じられている　先祖の霊
dead ancestors come back to visit the house during these

days and there are many customs to welcome them.

③One of them is a *bon-dana*. ④The *bon-dana* is a small

altar to welcome ancestors' spirits, on which the family put
～を迎える
o-hagi, rice balls covered with bean paste, and *somen*, very
豆の練りもので包んだご飯の玉(→おはぎ)
thin white noodles, as offerings to them. ⑤The table is
とても細く白い麺(→そうめん)　お供え
decorated with bamboo branches on each corner. ⑥People
～で飾りつけられている　竹の枝
also offer a horse-like figure made from cucumber and a
馬のような像　　　　　　　　　　　　　キュウリ
cow-like figure made from eggplant as transportation for
牛のような像　　　　　　　ナス　　　～のための乗り物として
the spirits. ⑦The horse is for their ancestors to come

quickly and the cow is for them to go back slowly because

many Japanese people don't like to see them leave.
　　　　　　　　　　　　　　　～が去るのを見たくない
⑧One fun summer event for the Japanese, the *Bon* Festival
楽しい夏の行事　　　　　　　　　　　　　　　盆踊り

Dance, held in parks or other open areas, was originally a
　　　　　　　　～で行なわれる　　　　空き地　　　　もともと
dance to welcome the spirits, too. ⑨It is thought that *Bon*

Festival Dance comes from the prayer dance Saint *Ippen*
　　　　　　　　～に由来する　　　念仏踊り　　　　一遍上人
started in the *Kamakura* period and later became connected
　　　　　　　　　　　　　　　　　　　　　　～と結びついた
with the *Bon* Festival. (see p.58)

---

16. お盆

①旧暦7月13〜15日の**お盆**は、日本人にとって正月と並ぶ、大切な季節行事です。②この日は、先祖の霊が家に戻ってくる日と考えられ、霊を迎え、もてなすためにさまざま習慣が伝えられてきました。

③その一つが**盆棚**です。④盆棚は霊をもてなすためのもので、小さな祭壇の上に先祖の霊が食べるためのおはぎやそうめんなどを供えます。⑤その四隅には竹を立てて飾りつけます。⑥そこに、キュウリでつくった馬やナスでつくった牛を供えますが、これは霊のために用意した乗り物です。⑦馬で一刻も早く来ていただき、牛で名残り惜しみながらゆっくりと帰っていただく、という意味があります。

⑧また、夏になると公園や空き地で行なわれ、夏の庶民の娯楽となっている**盆踊り**も、霊を迎えるための行事でした。⑨盆踊りは鎌倉時代に一遍上人が始めた念仏踊りが起源とされ、それがお盆と結びついたものと考えられています。

17. Moon Viewing

①Since Japan has four distinct seasons, most seasonal events
　　　　　　　　はっきりとした四季　　　多くの 季節行事
have much to do with the nature and climate of each season.
～と大いに関係がある　　　　　　　　気候
②Moon viewing is a typical example of this.
　　　　　　　　　代表的な例
③It is well-known that the moon is the most beautiful in the
　～はよく知られている
Northern hemisphere in September. ④This is because the
北半球で
moon is at its brightest in September due to the position of
　　　一番明るい　　　　　　　　～によって　～の位置
the sun and earth. ⑤Another reason is that the dry air flowing
　　　　　　　　　　　　　　　　　　　　　　　　　～から—に流れ込む
into Japan from China makes the sky clear and the moon
　　　　　　　　　　～を澄ませる
looks more beautiful. ⑥Moon viewing is an event where
より美しく見える
people enjoy the most beautiful moon of the year in the fall.

⑦Although the Chinese people started this event and
　～だけれども
introduced it into Japan, it is Japan's own custom to offer
～を—に伝えた
sweet rice dumplings and pampas grass while viewing the
団子　　　　　　　　ススキ
moon. ⑧Records show that in-season foods such as
　　　記録によると～だ　　　季節の食べ物
chestnuts, persimmons, taros, were also offered to the
栗　　　柿　　　里芋
moon in the *Edo* period. ⑨While customs differ from one
　　　　　　　　　　　　～ではあるが　　　異なる　地方によって

area to another, offering sweet rice dumplings and pampas

grass is common today.
一般的な

⑩The ears of pampas grass have been thought to be the
穂　　　　　　　　　　　　　～だと考えられてきた

symbol of fall in Japan since the old days. ⑪People say that
象徴　　　　　　　　　　　　　　　　　　　～といわれている

rice dumplings came to be offered to the moon because

they are similar in shape to the full moon. (see p.58)
形が～に似ている　　　　　満月

---

17. 月見

①日本の気候は、四季の変化がはっきりとしていることから、多くの季節行事は自然や季節感と深く関わっています。②その代表的なものの一つが月見です。

③北半球では、月は9月が一番きれいに見えることが知られています。④これは、太陽と地球の位置に関係し、月が一番明るく見えるからです。⑤また、日本では秋になると乾燥した空気が大陸から流れ込むため、空が澄み、月がいっそう美しく見えるのです。⑥月見は、この1年中で一番美しい秋の月を楽しむ行事です。

⑦月見は中国で始まり、日本に伝えられたとされていますが、ススキや月見団子を供えて月見をする習慣は、日本独自のものです。⑧江戸時代には季節の栗、柿、里芋といった季節の実りを供えたという記録もあります。⑨地方によって異なる習慣もありますが、現在は団子とススキを供えるのが一般的です。⑩日本では昔から、ススキの穂は秋を象徴する植物とされてきました。⑪また、団子はその形が満月に似ていることから、これらを月に供えるようになったと考えられています。

18. The Rooster Fair

①*Tori-no-ichi*, the Rooster Fair, is held on the Day of the
Rooster in November at shrines and temples located in *Kanto*
area mainly in *Tokyo*'s *Asakusa* district. ②Although it is a
fair, the only thing sold there is *engi-kumade*, or good-luck
bamboo rake charms. ③Good luck charms are attached to the
ceremonial rakes. ④The rake, a tool used to gather up fallen
leaves, reminds people of gathering up good luck and money
so it is considered a symbol of success for businesses. ⑤Those
who buy a good-luck bamboo rake charm return it to the shrine
the following year and buy another one to replace it. ⑥At that
time, people buy a bigger charm than the last year's and pray
for even more success in the coming year.

⑦Depending on the year, there are two or three Days of the
Rooster in November and the Rooster Fairs are held on
these days. ⑧The first fair is called the "first rooster" and
the second one is called the "second rooster". ⑨The third

fair is called the "third rooster" and legend has it that there
三の酉　　　　　　　　　　　〜という言い伝えがある

are frequent fires in the years with a "third rooster".
火事がよくある

⑩Even today, the Rooster Fair is crowded with people who
〜でにぎわう

come to get *engi-kumade*. ⑪Small rakes are about 20

centimeters long and the bigger ones are more than 1 meter.
20センチの長さ　　　　　　　　　　　　　　　　　1メートル

⑫Some big ones are sold for nearly 100,000 yen. (see p.59)

---

18. 酉の市

①「酉の市」は、11月の「酉の日」に、東京の浅草を中心として関東地方の神社や寺に立つ市です。②「市」といっても、酉の市で売られるのは「縁起熊手」と呼ばれるものだけ。③「縁起熊手」というのは、熊手を模したものに、縁起物を飾りつけたものです。④落ち葉などをかき集める道具である「熊手」は、福やお金をかき集めるとされ、縁起熊手は商売繁盛の象徴とされてきました。⑤この「縁起熊手」は次の年に神社に返して、新しいものに買い換えます。⑥そのときは前よりも大きく高価なものを買い、さらなる繁盛を願います。

⑦11月の酉の日は2回ないし3回あり、その日に合わせて酉の市が立ちます。⑧1回目の酉の市を一の酉、2回目を二の酉といいます。⑨3回目は三の酉ですが、三の酉まである年は、火事が多いという言い伝えがあります。

⑩今でも、酉の市は、「縁起熊手」を求めてやってくる多くの人々によってにぎわいます。⑪小さいものは20センチくらいですが、1メートルを超える大きなものもあります。⑫そうしたものは10万円近い値段がつけられていることもあります。

19. Winter Solstice Day

①*Toji*, or winter solstice day, is the day around December
<u>冬の至点の日(→冬至)</u>
22 with the shortest <u>amount</u> of daytime and the longest
量
amount of nighttime in the year. ②It was thought that
<u>~だと考えられていた</u>
animals and plants <u>grew weaker</u> around this time because
弱くなった
of the coldness and <u>lack of sunlight.</u>
~が欠けていること
③However; many people thought that this was a good day,

because the days <u>grew longer</u> from that time and that it was
長くなった
the starting point of <u>the Sun's movement.</u> ④<u>Since ancient</u>
太陽の運行   古来より
times, the Chinese people <u>have celebrated</u> the winter
~を祝ってきた
solstice day as <u>the beginning of the calendar</u>, and this <u>belief</u>
暦の起点として   信仰
entered Japan later.

⑤Most of <u>the annual events</u> in Japan <u>have something to do</u>
年中行事   ~と関係がある
<u>with</u> food. ⑥In the winter there is <u>the custom of</u> eating
~する習慣
pumpkin, <u>adzuki bean porridge</u>, *konnyaku*, and so on.
カボチャ 小豆粥
⑦What people eat <u>differs from one area to another</u> but
地域によって異なる
pumpkin is the most popular among the foods. ⑧It was

thought that eating pumpkin on the winter solstice day

kept people from having strokes and colds. ⑨Another
　　　　～が—するのを防ぐ　　　脳卒中　　風邪

important custom not to be forgotten is taking a yudzu
　　　　　忘れてはならない習慣　　　　　　柚子湯

bath. ⑩Taking a yudzu bath is good for chapped and
　　　　　　　　　　　　　　～によい　　　ひびとあかぎれ肌

cracked skin. ⑪People today, however, enjoy the bath more

for its fragrance of yudzu than for it benefits to their skin.
　～の香りのため　　　　　　　皮膚に対する効果のため

---

19. 冬至

①冬至とは、1年中でもっとも昼が短く夜が長い日で、12月の22日前後です。②寒さが増し、日が短くなるこの頃は、動植物の生命力が弱くなると考えられていました。

③その一方で、これから昼が長くなることから、太陽の運行の出発点である、めでたい日とも考えられてきました。④古来中国には、冬至は暦の起点として祝う習慣があり、これが日本に伝わったものです。

⑤日本の年中行事の多くは食べ物と結びついています。⑥冬至にはカボチャや小豆粥、コンニャクなどを食べます。⑦何を食べるかは地域による違いもあるのですが、なかでももっとも知られているのがカボチャです。⑧冬至にカボチャを食べると中風（脳卒中）になりにくくなり、風邪をひかなくなると考えられていました。⑨もう一つ、忘れてはならないのが「柚子湯」です。⑩これは、柚子を入れた風呂に入浴する習慣で、ひび、あかぎれに効果があると考えられていました。⑪最近は皮膚に対する効果よりも、柚子の香りを楽しみながら入浴する習慣として残っています。

20. Year-end Cleaning

① *Susu-harai* is when people clean their entire house at the
　　　　　　　　　　　　　　　　　　　　家じゅう　　　　　　年末に
end of the year, and they clean every corner of their house

including places usually missed by everyday cleaning. ② This
　　　　　　　　　　　　　　しそこなった　　日常の掃除
"year-end cleaning" is not only done in houses but in
　　　　　　　　　　　　～でされるだけでなく―ででも
companies and schools before the New Year holiday.
　　　　　　　　　　　　　　　　　正月休み
③ Year-end cleaning used to be done to welcome the *Toshigami-*
　　　　　　　　　　　　　　　　　　　　～を迎える　年神さま
sama god of the New Year and was also called *susu-osame.*

④ In the old days, people used firewood for cooking so the whole
　　昔には　　　　　　　　　　　　　薪
house would be covered with soot. ⑤ Because people cleaned the
　　　　　　　　　　　　　煤で汚れた
soot at that time, they called this cleaning *susu-harai,* which

meant clearing away soot. ⑥ This word, *susu-harai,* later came to
　　　　～を払うこと
be used for cleaning done at the end of the year.
～に使われるようになった
⑦ In the *Edo* period, the *Tokugawa* shogunate fixed the day
　　　　　　　　　　　　　徳川幕府　　　　　　　　　　　～の(ための)日
for *susu-osame* on December 13 and year-end cleaning was

done in *Edo-jo* castle on this day. ⑧ Some say that the
　　　　　江戸城　　　　　　　　　　　　　～という人もいる
custom of the public cleaning their entire house at the end
庶民が～を掃除する習慣

of the year started because of this.

⑨Nowadays, people tend to forget about the words *susu-*
<u>〜について忘れる傾向にある</u>
harai and *susu-osame* but they still <u>spend all day</u> cleaning
<u>丸一日を〜にかける</u>
every part of their offices or schools at the end of the year.
<u>〜のあらゆる場所</u>
⑩This is an important <u>annual event</u> where Japanese people
<u>年中行事</u>
wash away the "dirt" of the past year.
<u>過ぎ去る年の汚れを落とす</u>

---

20. 煤はらい

① 「**煤はらい**」とは、年末にふだん掃除できないような場所まで大がかりに掃除をすることです。②一般の家庭に限らず、職場や学校でも、正月休みに入る前に大掃除をします。

③これはもともと、新しい年の年神さまを迎えるに当たって住まいを清めることを目的とした行事で、「**煤納め**」とも呼ばれていました。④昔は煮炊きに薪を使っていたので、家の中は煤で汚れてしまいました。⑤これを掃除するという意味で、「煤はらい」という言葉が生まれました。⑥それが、やがて年末の大掃除を指すようになったのです。

⑦江戸時代には、徳川幕府が12月13日を「煤納め」の日と定め、江戸城の大掃除を行ないました。⑧これが庶民の間に広まり、年末に大掃除をする習慣が生まれたという説もあります。

⑨最近、「煤はらい」や「煤納め」といった言葉は忘れられつつありますが、年末になると職場でも学校でも、丸一日かけて丹念に隅々まで掃除する人々の姿が見られます。⑩年末の大掃除は日本人にとって、一年の汚れを落とすための、大切な年中行事なのです。

21. Year-end Party

①A *bonen-kai*, or year-end party, like cherry blossom viewing, is one of the annual events many Japanese people look forward to. ②Although today's *bonen-kai* is a party where people enjoy drinking with relatives, friends or co-workers, it had more to do with religion in the old days. ③Since ancient times, the Japanese people have thought that spirits of their ancestors come back on New Year's Eve. ④In the *Heian* period, *mitama-matsuri* festivals were held to welcome the spirits on New Year's Eve. ⑤Shrines today keep following this tradition by having festivals for the spirits. ⑥In the *Muromachi* period, court nobles enjoyed *toshi-wasure*, or forget-the-year parties to forget the last year. ⑦At the parties, they drank and made *renga*, linked verses, from the New Year's Eve until the morning of New Year's Day. ⑧However, they were not like today's *bonen-kai*, where people drink and get excited. ⑨In the old days,

parties were held in a more tasteful tone.
　　　　　　　　　　もっと風流な調子で

⑩It is said that the custom of drinking together and talking
　　　　　　　　　　　　～する習慣

about what they did in the past year began among
　　　彼らがしたこと

employees in the urban areas after the _Meiji_ or _Taisho_
雇われ人　　　都市部　　　　　　　　　明治・大正時代

period. ⑪The name _bonen-kai_ comes from the old name
　　　　　　　　　　　　　　　　～に由来する

toshi-wasure, or forget-the-year party.

---

21. 忘年会

①**忘年会**は、花見と並んで多くの日本人が楽しみに待つ行事の一つです。②現在の忘年会は、親戚や友人、職場の仲間が集まってお酒を飲みながら楽しむ宴会ですが、時代をさかのぼると、宗教的な意味合いが強いものだったようです。

③古来、日本では大晦日の夜には先祖の霊が戻ってくると考えられていました。④平安時代、大晦日に行なわれていた「霊祭り」は、霊を迎えるために行なわれていたものです。⑤現在も、大晦日に霊祭りを行なう神社がありますが、これはその名残です。⑥室町時代になると、公家のあいだで旧年のよくないことを忘れてしまうようにという「**年忘れ**」の宴を楽しむようになりました。⑦これは大晦日から元日の朝にかけて、お酒を飲みながら連歌を詠うものです。⑧現在の忘年会のようにお酒を飲んで騒ぐというようなものではありませんでした。⑨それはなかなか風流な雰囲気のものでした。⑩現在のように、一年の労をねぎらいながら酒を酌み交わす習慣は、明治・大正期以降に都市部の勤め人の間で生まれたようです。⑪「忘年会」という言葉は、「年忘れ」に由来したものです。

22. Ringing Out the Old Year

①December 31 is called *o-misoka* day. ②The last day of each
　　　　　　　　　　　　　　大晦日

month is called *misoka* day, so that people came to call the last
　　　　　　　　　晦日　　　　　　　　　　　　　　　　　　～を—と呼ぶ

day of the year *o-misoka* day which means big *misoka day.*

③The last night of the year on *o-misoka* day is called *jo-ya* night.
　　　　　　　　　　　　　　　　　　　　　　　　　　　　　　除夜

④*Jo-ya* night means "the night to remove last year's evil".
　　　　　　　　　　　　　　　　　～を除く　　　　　　　災い

⑤On the lunisolar calendar, a new day started with sunset , so
　　太陰太陽暦では　　　　　　　　　　　　　　　　　　　日暮れ

that people thought *jo-ya* night was the beginning of a new year.

⑥The *Toshigami-sama* god came down on *jo-ya* night. ⑦It
　　　　年神さま

was a tradition for people to stay up all night to welcome the
　　　　　　　　　　　　　　　一晩中寝ない　　　　　　～を迎える

god. ⑧Today people follow this tradition when they make
　　　　　　　　　　　　～に従う

first visit to shrines or temples at midnight on *o-misoka*,
初詣をする

although many of them are not even aware of the tradition.
　　　　　　　　　　　　　　　～を気づきさえしない

⑨At temples, bells to ring out the old year are rung at
　　　　　　　　鐘　　鳴らして旧年を送る(→除夜)　　鳴らされる

midnight on *o-misoka* day. ⑩This tradition was introduced

to Japan from Sung China in the *Kamakura* period. ⑪The
　　　　　　　　宋代の中国

bells are rung 108 times from midnight to the morning of

New Year's Day. ⑫ One of the opinions is that the number
108 is the number of human desires which is thought to be
　　　　　　　　　　　　　　　　　煩悩
108. ⑬ By ringing the bell the same amount of times as
　　　　～によって
human desires, it is believed that the sins of the old year
　　　　　　　　　　　　　　　　　　　　　　旧年の罪
can be washed away and that people can turn a new leaf to
洗い流されることができる　　　　　　　　　　　　　心機一転する
ring in the New Year. (see p.59)
新しい年を迎える

(see p.59)

---

22. 年越し

①12月31日を**大晦日**（おおみそか）といいます。②晦日が月の最終日を指すことから、1年の最終日を大晦日と呼ぶようになりました。③この大晦日の夜が「**除夜**（じょや）」です。

④除夜とは、「旧年の災いを除く夜」という意味です。⑤太陰太陽暦（旧暦）が使われていた時代には、日暮れに新しい1日が始まるとされていたため、除夜は新しい年の始まりと考えられていました。⑥除夜には年神さまが降りてきます。⑦人々は除夜には寝ないで年神さまをお迎（むか）えするのがしきたりでした。⑧現在は多くの人が、大晦日の真夜中から神社や寺に初詣に出かけますが、これはその名残りでしょう。

⑨寺では、大晦日の真夜中から除夜の鐘を鳴らします。⑩この習慣は宋代の中国から鎌倉時代の日本に伝わったものです。⑪大晦日の深夜から元日の朝にかけて108回、鐘がつかれます。⑫この108という数字については、諸説ありますが、その一つは、108あるとされる人間の煩悩（ぼんのう）を表しているというものです。⑬煩悩の数だけ鐘をつくことで前年の罪を洗い流し、あらたな気持ちで新しい年を迎えることを、象徴しています。

盆棚と迎え火

The Small Altar to Welcome Ancestors' Spirits and the Welcome Fire

お盆には、先祖の霊を迎えるため、盆棚をつくります。キュウリで作った馬は、霊をお迎えする乗り物、ナスで作った牛は霊が帰るときの乗り物です。

For the Bon Festival, people prepare a small table to welcome their ancestors' spirits. The horse-like figure made from cucumber is transportation for the spirits to come and the cow-like figure made from eggplant is transportation for the spirits to leave.

夕方、迎え火をたきます。先祖の霊は、その煙に乗って来ると信じられていました。

People make a welcome fire in the evening. They believed that ancestors' spirits come with the smoke.

月見

Moon Viewing

ススキを飾り、月にお団子をお供えして、月見を楽しみます。

People enjoy viewing the moon while offering sweet rice dumplings and pampas grass to the moon.

酉の市
^{とり} ^{いち}

The Rooster Fair

酉の市の日には、神社や寺の境内に、
縁起熊手を売る屋台が所狭しと並び
ます。

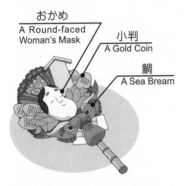

おかめ
A Round-faced Woman's Mask

小判
A Gold Coin

鯛
A Sea Bream

At the Rooster Fair, the grounds of shrines and temples are crowded with stalls selling good-luck bamboo rake charms.

年越し

Ringing Out the Old Year

一般の家庭では、大晦日の夜に
家族そろってソバを食べる習慣
があります。細くて長いソバは長
寿の象徴と考えられているからで
す。

It is a common custom for families to eat long, thin brown soba noodles together on New Year's Eve. People believe that soba noodles are a symbol for a long life because they are long and thin.

Calendars / 暦

There are three calendars in the world: the lunar calendar, based on the phases of the moon, the solar calendar, based on the movement of the sun and the lunisolar calendar, which is a combination of the two.

Today, the solar calendar, or the Gregorian calendar, is used all over the world. Japan used to use the lunisolar calendar but adopted the solar calendar in 1873, the 6th year of *Meiji*.

One year on the lunar calendar has 354 days because this calendar is based on the phases of the moon, which run in 29.5-day cycles. Because of this, the lunar calendar slowly becomes out of sync with the seasons. To correct this, seven leap months are inserted into every 19-year span. Those years end up having 13 months which keeps the calendar year linked to the seasons.

暦には月の満ち欠けをもとにした太陰暦と、太陽の運行をもとにした太陽暦と、それを組み合わせた太陰太陽暦があります。現代の暦は太陽暦（グレゴリオ暦）で、世界共通です。日本では明治6（1873）年にこれを採用するまで太陰太陽暦を用いていました。

太陰暦は月の満ち欠けを基準としますが、その周期は29.5日なので1年は354日となります。そのため、季節がずれてしまいます。それを補正するため、19年に7回の閏月をはさみ、その年を1年を13ヵ月とすることで補正した暦です。

Traditions for Lifetime Events

第２章

人生のしきたり

23. Weddings and Religion

①Today, the Japanese people mainly have *Shinto*-style
weddings or Christian-style ones. ②Also, there are
weddings in public regardless of religion. ③According to a
poll in the 2008 bridal magazine, *Zexy*, 64 percent of
couples had Christian-style weddings, 18 percent had
Shinto-style, 16 percent had weddings in public, and 2
percent had other kinds of weddings. ④Buddhist-style
weddings are rarely held and they were among the other
kinds of weddings in the poll above. ⑤On the other hand,
about 49 percent of the Japanese people believe in *Shinto*,
about 45 percent believe in Buddhism, about 1 percent
believe in Christianity, and about 5 percent believe in other
religions or have no religion at all.

⑥This poll shows that most of the couples who believe in
Shinto or Buddhism and who don't have a religion had
Christian-style weddings.

⑦As a result, more than half of the weddings are held in
　　　　　　　　　　　　　　　　　　　　　　　　　　　　　行なわれる
the Christian style. ⑧It is needless to say that, *Shinto*-style
　　　　　　　　　　　　～であることはいうまでもない
weddings are the most uniquely Japanese. ⑨However, it
　　　　　　　　　　　一番日本特有のものである
was established in early 20th century.

---

23. 結婚式と宗教

①現在、日本の**結婚式**は主に**神道式**と**キリスト教式**で行なわれています。②そのほか、宗教と無関係に行なう**人前結婚式**もあります。③2008年に結婚情報雑誌『ゼクシィ』が行なった調査では、その比率は、キリスト教式が64パーセント、神前式が18パーセント、人前式が16パーセント、その他が2パーセントという結果が出ています。④**仏前式**はごくわずかで、その他に含まれます。⑤一方、各宗教の信者の比率は、神道が約49パーセント、仏教約45パーセント、キリスト教約1パーセント、その他が約5パーセントとなっています。

⑥この結果から、多くの神道や仏教の信者、あるいは宗教を持たない人々が、キリスト教式で挙式していることがわかります。⑦このように、結婚式の半数以上はキリスト教式で行なわれています。⑧一番日本的であるのは神道式であることは、いうまでもありません。⑨ただし、それも20世紀前半から、日本で発明された方式にすぎません。

24. Marriage

①Marriages in Japan have changed little by little over time.
婚姻　　　　　　　　　　　　　　　少しずつ　　　時代とともに

②Among the noble class in the *Heian* period, it is
貴族階級では

well-known that husband and wife lived apart and that the
〜だということがよく知られている　　　　離れて住んだ

husband went to and from his wife's house. ③It became
〜を行き来する

usual for couples to live together in the husband's house
ふつうの　　　　　　　一緒に住む

among the *samurai* class because there were many cases
武家階級では

that couples living far from each other got married.
互いに遠く離れて住んでいる

④This living-together marriage became popular partly
一緒に住む形の婚姻

because it was important to continue the family line from
〜も理由の一つとして　　　　　　　　父から息子への家系

father to son. ⑤Therefore the wife had to leave her family
〜から離れる

to become a member of her husband's family, and she could

not be free from this family.
〜から解放されない

⑥In Japanese, phrases like "join his family as a wife" and
妻として家に入る

"welcome a wife to my family" are often used even today
家に妻を迎える

instead of "get married". ⑦These phrases come from these
〜のかわりに　　　　　　　　　　　　〜に由来する

old customs.

⑧Japan's period of high growth began around 1960 and
　日本の高度成長期

many young people left their parents in farm villages to
　　　　　　　　　　　　　　　　　　　　　　　農村

start to live in big cities. ⑨As a result, couples who started
　　　　　　　　　　　　　　　その結果

families away from their parents increased, and their ideas
両親と離れて所帯を持つ　　　　　　　　　　増えた

about marriage shifted from the continuing of the family
結婚に対する考え　　変化した　　家系を継続させること

line to marriages for themselves.
　　　　自分たちのための結婚

---

24. 婚姻

①日本の婚姻(こんいん)の形は、歴史とともに変ってきました。②平安時代の貴族社会では、夫が妻の家に通う通(かよ)い式(しき)だったことが知られています。③その後、遠方の家同士の婚姻関係が多くなったことから、武家社会では嫁入り婚が広がりました。

④日本の嫁入り婚は、男親から息子に受け継がれる家系を守ることも関係して普及したようです。⑤そのため、妻は実家を捨てて夫の家の人間にならなければならず、妻は嫁(とつ)いだ先の家に束縛(そくばく)されることになりました。

⑥日本語では今でも、「結婚する」の代わりに「お嫁に行く」とか、「嫁をもらう」といった表現が多く使われます。⑦これはそうした習俗の名残りです。

⑧1960年頃から経済が高度成長期を迎えると、多くの若者が農村の親元を離れて都会で暮らすようになりました。⑨その結果、親と別に所帯を持つ夫婦が増え、結婚に対する考え方も家のための結婚から個人のための結婚へ変化しました。

25. Matchmaking Meetings

①*Miai*, or matchmaking meeting, is an event in which a
結婚仲介の会
go-between called *nako-do* brings together a man and a
仲介者   ～を引き合わせる
woman who are of marrying age.
結婚適齢期の
②In the Japanese society, people have had the freedom to
開放的に恋愛をする自由があった
love openly since early times. ③Especially in farm villages
昔から   農村
and fishing villages, it was common for young people to
漁村   ～が―するのが一般的だった
meet at the *Bon* Festival Dance in summer or autumn
盆踊り
festivals, fall in love and then get married. ④High ranking
恋愛する   結婚する   身分の高い
samurai or rich townspeople, however, thought much of
武士   町人   一方   ～を重んじた
their parents' opinions and family line when they wanted to
親の意思   家系
marry. ⑤Those upper-class people began to have *miai* to
上流の
look for the right wife for their family. ⑥It was in the *Meiji*
～を探す ～にふさわしい嫁   ～というのは明治時代だった
period that the general public also began to have *miai*.
庶民
⑦Most of the people in the *Meiji* period and before World
第二次世界大戦
War II in the *Showa* period got married to a person they

met by *miai*.

⑧After World War II, many people <u>got married for love</u>,
恋愛のために結婚した

rather than *miai*. ⑨However, *miai* is still a good way to find
〜よりもむしろ

<u>a marriage partner</u> for young people today <u>with no</u>
結婚相手

<u>opportunities</u> to find a partner <u>in their everyday life</u>.
〜する機会がない　　　　　　　　日常生活で

25. 見合い

①**見合い**とは、**仲人**と呼ばれる紹介者が仲介に立って、結婚適
齢期の男女を引き合わせるものです。

②日本社会は、歴史的にみても恋愛はかなり自由でした。③特
に農村や漁村では、夏の盆踊りや秋の祭で男女が出会い、恋愛
の末に結婚するというのが一般的でした。④一方、身分が高い
武士や裕福な町人は、結婚にあたり、親の意思や家柄が重んじ
られました。⑤見合いは、そうした江戸時代の上流階級の間で
「家にふさわしい嫁」を探すための手段として行なわれるよう
になりました。⑥それが庶民の間に広まるのは、明治時代にな
ってからのことです。⑦明治から昭和の戦前にかけては、見合
い結婚が主流でした。

⑧戦後、再び**恋愛結婚**が主流になりました。⑨現在でも異性と
の出会いが少ない環境にいる若者にとって、見合いは結婚相手
を探す大きなチャンスの一つとなっています。

26. Engagement Presents

①*Yui-no* is a ceremony before the wedding to celebrate the
結婚式　　　　　　　　　　〜を祝福する
joining of two families; bridegroom gives engagement
〜が結びつくこと　　　　　　　　　　　　結納金
money and other engagement presents, such as food and
　　　　　　　　　　結納品
sake, to the bride's family. ②Usually a matchmaker, who

mediates two families, carries the whole *yui-no* ceremony;
両家を仲介する
the matchmaker hands a gift to the bride instead of the
　　　　　　　　　　　　　　　　　　　　　〜の代わりに
bridegroom and hands a return gift to the bridegroom

instead of the bride.

③In the old days, it was a custom for the bridegroom to

visit the bride's family with food and *sake* and eat and

drink together before the wedding.

④It became popular for couples to live together in the
　　　　　　　　　　　　　　　　　　夫の家で一緒に暮らす
husband's house, called *yome-iri-kon*, among the *samurai*

class between the civil war and *Edo* period. ⑤They began
　　　　　戦国時代から江戸時代にかけて
to exchange expensive things and large sums of money
　　　　　　　　高価な　　　　　　　　　大金
according to their family status. ⑥However, this was held
　　　　　　　　　　家の格式

only among the *samurai* and merchant classes.
〜のあいだでだけ

⑦It was in the *Meiji* and *Taisho* period that this custom

became popular among the general public. ⑧As the
〜するにつれ

ceremonies concerned with marriage get to be simplified,
　　　〜に関係する→まつわる　　　　　　　　　簡素化された

couples who do not exchange engagement presents are

recently increasing.
最近　　　増えている

---

26. 結納

①**結納**(ゆいのう)とは、結婚に先立ち、男性側が「**結納金**」や酒肴(しゅこう)などの「**結納品**」を女性側に納め、親族となることを祝う儀式です。②仲人が、新郎と新婦の間に入り、結納の金品と結納返しの受け渡しをし、結納の儀式を取り仕切るのが普通です。

③古くは、結婚が決まると婿(むこ)が酒と肴(さかな)を携(たずさ)えて嫁の家を訪問し、酒を酌(く)み交わすしきたりがありました。

④戦国時代から江戸時代にかけては、武家社会でいわゆる嫁入り婚が盛んになりました。⑤同時に、家の格式に合った豪華な品々やお金を交換するようになりました。⑥しかし、武家や商家など、ごく限られた人々のあいだで行なわれていただけでした。

⑦これが一般に広まるのは、明治・大正の頃からです。⑧結婚にまつわる儀式が簡素化されるにつれ、最近は結納を取り交わさないカップルが多くなりました。

27. Shinto-style Weddings

①Nowadays there are a large number of young couples who
かなりの数の
have Christian-style weddings. ②However, as for weddings
キリスト教式の結婚式   ～といえば
in Japan, people must remember *Shinto*-style weddings, in
神道式の結婚式
which the couples take a marriage vow in front of the god
結婚を誓う   ～の前で
of *Shinto*.

③In *Shinto*-style weddings, the *Shinto* priest first purifies
神主   ～をお祓いする
the couple with *o-asa*, a stick with many pieces of thin
paper. ④Next, the priest says a *Shinto* prayer, inform the
祝詞をとなえる   ～に―を報告する
god of their marriage, and then the couple do the three-
結婚   三三九度の盃をかわす
times-three exchange of wedding cups. ⑤After that, they
exchange wedding rings, which comes from the Western
結婚指輪   西欧の習慣
custom. ⑥Last, they take a marriage vow and offer a
branch of a holy tree to the god.
玉串を奉げる
⑦People may think this *Shinto*-style wedding is a
traditional Japanese one from ancient times, but it is
古来からの
actually not so old. ⑧After Prince *Yoshihito*, later Emperor
嘉仁親王   後の大正天皇

Taisho, took a marriage vow in front of *Amaterasu-omikami*, the goddess of the sun, *Shinto*-style weddings
太陽の女神
became popular among upper-class people and later among
上流階級の人々
the general public. ⑨Before that, Japanese weddings only
庶民
had a drinking party which had nothing to do with religion.
酒宴　　　　　　　　　　　〜と関係がない　　　　　　宗教

(see p.84)

27. 神前結婚

①最近はキリスト教式で挙式する若者が圧倒的に多くなりました。②しかし，日本的な結婚式といえば、やはり神道の神に結婚を誓う、**神前結婚**です。

③神前結婚は神主が大麻でお祓いをすることから始まります。
④次に神主が祝詞をとなえたのち、新郎・新婦は神さまに結婚の報告をして、三三九度の杯をかわします。⑤ここで指輪を交換しますが、これは西欧の習慣から取り入れられたものです。
⑥そして、神さまに結婚の誓いをのべ、玉串を奉げます。

⑦ただし、この神前結婚は、日本古来の伝統であるように思われていますが、実はそれほど古いものではありません。⑧明治33年に嘉仁親王（後の大正天皇）が天照大神の前で結婚を誓ったことがきっかけとなり、上流階級から庶民へと広がったものです。⑨それ以前の日本の結婚式は、酒宴が中心で宗教と関係なく行なわれていました。

28. Drinking from Wedding Cups

①*San-san-ku-do*, drinking from wedding cups, is a ceremony in which the couple drinks *sake* from three cups, a small cup, a medium-sized one, and a large one. ②These cups are placed on top of one another and the couple drinks each with three sips so they both take nine sips in total. ③In ancient China, 3 was thought to be a lucky number according to the doctrine of the five natural elements of the positive and negative. ④The Chinese people hated the number 10 because it was the highest number and could only be reduced. ⑤Therefore 9 was the best positive number for them. ⑥As a result, the Japanese people also began to call their custom of drinking *sake* in three cups, taking three sips from each cup, *san-san-ku-do*. ⑦In the *Muromachi* period, it was one of the rules of behavior for the *samurai* class but it is held only at weddings today. ⑧At weddings, the bridegroom drinks from the first cup

followed by the bride. ⑨Next, the bride drinks from the
　　　　　　　　　　　 続いて(〜が飲む)　新婦

second cup followed by the bridegroom. ⑩Finally, the

bridegroom drinks from the third cup, again followed by

the bride. ⑪As a rule, they pretend to drink on the first and
　　　　　　作法として　　　　 〜するふりをする

second sips and drink it all on the third sip. (see p.84)
　　　　　　　　　 飲み干す

(see p.84)

---

28. 三三九度

①三三九度とは大中小、三つの盃を用いて酒を飲み合う儀式
です。②盃は三重に重ねられており、一つの盃で３回ずつ計９
回飲み合います。

③古来、中国では陰陽五行説から、三は吉の数とされていま
した。④また、十は数字の頂点ですが欠けるしかない数字とし
て忌み嫌われていました。⑤そのため、九が最高の陽数とされ
ていました。⑥それにちなんで、三つの盃で３回ずつ酒を飲む
習慣を「三三九度」と呼びました。⑦室町時代には武家の作法
として取り入れられましたが、現在は婚礼だけの儀式となり、
残っています。

⑧結婚式では、一つ目の盃では新郎→新婦の順に飲みます。⑨二
つ目の盃では新婦→新郎の順。⑩三つ目の盃では新郎→新婦の
順に、交互に飲みます。⑪飲み方の作法としては、２回口をつ
けるだけにとどめ、３回目に飲み干すことになっています。

29. The Seventh Night

①The Japanese people have believed that the *Ubugami-sama* god protects their babies when they are born.
産神さま
~を守る

②The *Ubugami-sama* god left seven days after the baby was born
帰る

and people thought of the baby as a human child from that
~を—とみなした

day. ③Therefore the Japanese people called this day the

o-shichi-ya night, the seventh night, and it has been a
お七夜

custom to celebrate this night since ancient times.
~を祝う   昔から

④On the *o-shichi-ya* night, people invite their relatives and
~を—に招待する   親戚

neighbors to their house and treat them to a good dinner
近所の人たち   ~にご馳走をふるまう

such as *seki-han*, rice boiled with adzuki beans, and a
たとえば   ~と炊かれた   小豆

whole sea bream. ⑤At that dinner, the baby's family writes
尾頭付きの鯛

the baby's name on a piece of paper, and sticks it on a
紙に赤ちゃんの名前を書く(→命名書)

Shinto or Buddhist altar to introduce the name. ⑥At this
神棚や仏壇

event, the baby gets his or her own name as a human being.
人間として

⑦*O-shichi-ya* is the night to celebrate it.

⑧Other than that, there are many customs on the *o-shichi-*
そのほかでは

ya night. ⑨For example, taking the baby to the bathroom,
　　　　　　　たとえば　　　　　　　 ～を―に連れて行くこと　　便所

which is called *secchin-mairi,* is held around the country.
　　　　　　　　　　　　　　　　　　　　　　　　　　　　　各地で

⑩This is because people thought the *Ubugami-sama* god

was also the god of the bathroom.
　　　　便所の神さま

---

29. お七夜

①赤ちゃんが生まれるときには、産神さまが守ってくれると信
じられてきました。②産神さまは出産から7日目に帰ってし
まい、その日から赤ちゃんは人間の子供として認められるので
す。③そこで、昔からこの日を**お七夜**と呼び、お祝いをする習
慣がありました。

④お七夜には、赤飯や鯛の尾頭付きなどのご馳走を用意して
親戚や近所の人を招き、もてなします。⑤このときに、神棚や
仏前に**命名書**を貼り、子供の名前を披露します。⑥これをもっ
て、赤ちゃんは人間の子供として名前を持つことになります。
⑦お七夜はそのお祝いでもあります。

⑧そのほかにも、お七夜にはさまざまな習慣があります。⑨た
とえば、お七夜に便所にお参りする「**雪隠参り**」という習慣が、
各地に伝えられています。⑩それは、産神さまは便所の神さま
とも考えられていたからです。

30. Baby's First Visit to a Shrine

①The Japanese people take their new-born baby to the
Ujigami-sama god, a protecting god, about one month after
the baby is born. ②There, people pray to the god to protect
their baby and his or her healthy growth. ③This is called,
o-miya-mairi, a baby's first visit to a shrine.
④Generally, people take a baby boy when he is thirty-two
days old and a baby girl when she is thirty-three days old.
⑤The Japanese people thought that the mother was unclean
for some time after childbirth and that this period was over
after that time. ⑥Therefore, these are the first days a
mother can visit a shrine after she has the baby. ⑦On their
way to the shrine, the baby is held not by the mother but by
the grandmother because the mother is not strong enough
yet. ⑧At the shrine, it is a custom to write in red ink a
Chinese character meaning big, small, or dog on the
forehead of the baby. ⑨In the old days, people used to write

a *batsu* mark (×) with kitchen soot on the forehead of a
台所の煤
baby to keep off evil, and this was called *ayatsuko*. ⑩This
魔よけする
custom was taken up because people thought that the *batsu*
始められた
mark had the power to keep away evil and that kitchen soot

held the power of the house god. (see p.84)
持った

---

30. お宮参り

①赤ちゃんが生まれて約１ヵ月ほどすると、赤ちゃんをつれて氏神さまにお参りにいきます。②赤ちゃんが神の加護のもと、健やかに成長することを祈ります。③これが**お宮参り**です。
④普通は、男の子が生後32日、女の子は生後33日とされています。⑤この日は母親の「お産の血の忌み」が明ける日です。⑥そのため、産後初めて神社にお参りできる日でもあります。
⑦お宮参りに行くとき、母親でなく姑が赤ちゃんを抱くのは、産後の母親の体の負担を軽くするためです。
⑧お宮参りをするときに、赤ちゃんの額に紅で「大」、「小」、「犬」といった文字を書く習慣があります。⑨これはもともと魔よけで「**アヤツコ**」などと呼ばれ、かまどの煤で「×」を書くものでした。⑩「×」には魔よけの意味が、かまどの煤は家の神さまの霊力があると信じられていたことから生まれた習慣です。

31. A Baby's First Food

①Babies usually have only milk or some juice until they
_{〜までは}
are old enough to eat baby food, which is around 100 days.
_{成長して〜するようになる}　_{離乳食}　_{およそ〜}

②*O-kui-zome*, the baby's first food ceremony, is held at this
_{行なわれる}
time.

③This ceremony is named the "first food ceremony", but

the baby does not actually eat. ④This ceremony is held to

pray for the baby to have enough to eat throughout his or her
_{〜が—するように祈る}　_{彼あるいは彼女の長い人生を通して}
long life.

⑤People set a small table with one cup of soup and three
_{用意する お膳}　_{一汁}　_{三菜}
side dishes such as a whole grilled fish, like sea bream,
_{尾頭付きの焼き魚}　_鯛
boiled food, pickled vegetables, soup, and rice. ⑥There is a
_{煮物}　_{香の物}　_汁　_{ご飯}
small stone, too.

⑦They move the food to the baby's mouth and pretend to
_{〜を—にもっていく}　_{〜するふりをする}
feed the baby. ⑧The oldest person, usually a grandparent is
_{〜に食べさせる}　_{祖父母}
chosen for this role. ⑨Generally, a woman is chosen for a
_{この役割に選ばれる}
baby boy and a man is chosen for a baby girl.
_{男の赤ちゃん}　_{女の赤ちゃん}

⑩Next, they pretend to <u>let the baby</u> lick the small stone.
　　　　　　　　　　～になめさせる

⑪This act is called *ha-gatame*, <u>hardening the teeth</u>, and, by
　この行為　　　　　　　　　　　歯をかたくすること

doing this, people pray for the baby to have strong teeth

like a stone. (see p.85)

---

31. お食い初め

①赤ちゃんは生後約 100 日程度を過ぎると、離乳食を食べられるほどに成長します。②この時期に行なわれるのが、「**お食い初め**」です。

③「お食い初め」といっても実際に食べさせるわけではありません。④「一生食べることに困らないように」という願いを込めて行なう儀式です。

⑤尾頭付きの鯛などの焼き魚、煮もの、香の物、汁、ご飯の一汁三菜のお膳を用意します。⑥お膳には、小石も用意しておきます。

⑦このお膳の食べ物を赤ちゃんの口にもっていき、食べさせるマネをします。⑧この役割は祖父母など、身近にいる年長者から選びます。⑨男の子には女性、女の子には男性とされています。

⑩そして、小石を赤ちゃんになめさせるまねをします。⑪これは「**歯がため**」と呼ばれ、石のように丈夫な歯が生えるようにという願いを込めたものです。

32. Festival for Children Aged Seven, Five, and Three

①In Japan, it is a tradition for children who turn three, five,
〜が—するというしきたりがある
or seven that year to visit a shrine in their best clothes on
その年に　　　　　　　　　　　　　　晴れ着を着て
November 15. ②Today, only girls aged three or seven and
boys aged five take part in it.
〜に参加する
③This tradition comes from several ceremonies that were
〜に由来する　　　　　　伝統的な儀式　行なわれてきた
held around the country. ④Ceremonies such as, *kami-oki*, in
各地で
which children, who had their heads shaved until then,
それまで頭を剃っていた
started to grow their hair, *hakama-gi*, in which they wore a
髪を伸ばす
hakama, a Japanese male skirt, for the first time, and *obi-*
男のスカート
toki, in which they changed clothes from *kimono* with strings
紐付きの着物
to one with an *obi* for adults. ⑤Each of these was a ceremony
帯を巻く着物
to celebrate the turning-points of a child's growth.
節目　　　　　　　　　子どもの成長
⑥The festival for children aged seven comes from a custom
called *nanatsu-go-iwai*. ⑦In the old days, people thought
昔には
that children under the age of seven were not grown up yet
7歳に満たない子ども　　　　　　まだ〜しない
and were protected by the gods. ⑧Children became a
〜によって守られていた

member of society at the age of seven and visited the
社会の一員

Ujigami-sama god at that time and this is called *nanatsu-go-*

iwai. ⑨In the *Meiji* and *Taisho* periods, *kami-oki*, *hakama-*

gi, *obi-toki*, and *nanatsugo-iwai* came together and became
一緒になる

popular around the country as *shichi-go-san*, the festival for
七五三

children aged seven, five, and three. (see p.85)

---

32. 七五三

①日本には子供が 3 歳、5 歳、7 歳を迎えた年の 11 月 15 日に、晴れ着を着て神社にお参りするしきたりがあります。②現在は女の子は 3 歳と 7 歳のとき、男の子は 5 歳とされています。③そのもととなったのは、各地に伝統的に伝わる儀式でした。④3 歳のとき、それまで剃っていた髪を伸ばす「**髪置き**」、5 歳のとき、初めて袴をはかせる「**袴着**」、そして 7 歳のとき、それまでの紐付きの着物から、帯を巻く本格的な着物に替える「**帯解き**」といったものです。⑤それぞれ、子供の成長の節目となる年齢に祝う儀式でした。

⑥7 歳の祝いのもとになったのは、「**七つ子祝い**」という風習でした。⑦古来、7 歳に満たない子供はまだ不安定で神さまの庇護のもとにあると考えられていました。⑧7 歳になると、改めて社会的な存在になりますが、その節目として氏神さまにお参りするのが、七つ子祝いです。⑨明治・大正以降、「髪置き」、「袴着」、「帯解き」、「七つ子祝い」がまとまり、**七五三**として全国に広がったと考えられています。

33. The Coming-of-age Ceremony

①In Japan, the second Sunday of January is the coming-of-age
<small>成年に達する儀式の日(→成人の日)</small>
ceremony day, which celebrates young people who will become
<small>〜を祝う</small>
adults that year. ②People become adults at the age of 20 under
<small>成人</small> <small>20歳で</small>
Japanese civil law today and are thought of as grown-ups.
<small>日本の民法のもとで</small> <small>〜としてみなされる</small> <small>大人</small>
③However, children from the age of 15 to 17 in *kazoe-doshi*, the
<small>15歳から17歳の</small>
calendar year, were thought of as adults before the *Edo* period.
<small>数え年で</small>
④A *heko* party, or Japanese loincloth party for men, and a *yumoji*
<small>日本の褌</small>
party, or Japanese waistcloth party for women, were popular
<small>日本の腰巻</small>
among the general public as ceremonies in which children
<small>庶民</small> <small>儀式として</small>
became adults. ⑤Men began to wear a loincloth and woman
began to wear a waistcloth for the first time when they became
adults. ⑥People had a custom of giving loincloths or waistcloths
<small>〜する習慣があった</small>
to young people who were thought of as adults. ⑦A *heko* party
or a *yumoji* party was held to celebrate their coming-of-age.

⑧A *genpuku*, or *eboshi-gi* party, in which men put on a
<small>〜をかぶる</small>
crown for the first time, and a *kane-tsuke* party, in which
<small>冠</small>

women painted their teeth black, were also held mainly
歯を黒く塗る　　　　　　　　　　　　　　　～のあいだを中心に
among the noble class and the *samurai* class as the
貴族階級　　　　　　　　武士階級
ceremonies in which children became adults.

⑨The Japanese government made the coming-of-age
日本政府　　　　　　　　～を—とする
ceremony a day for local governments to hold such
地方自治体
traditional ceremonies around the country since 1947.

---

33. 成人式

①1月の第2日曜日は、その年に成人を迎える若者を祝う「**成人の日**」です。②現在の日本の民法では、20歳で成人となり、大人として認められます。③しかし，江戸時代以前には数え年15歳から17歳くらいで成人とみなされました。

④子供から大人になる儀式として、庶民の間で広く行なわれていたのが、男子の「褌祝い」や女子の「湯文字祝い」です。⑤成人になって初めて男子は褌、女子は腰巻を身につけることになっていました。⑥そのため、成人として認められると褌や腰巻を贈られる習慣がありました。⑦「褌祝い」と「湯文字祝い」はこれを祝うものです。

⑧また、貴族や武家を中心に、成人となるための儀式として、男子が初めて冠をかぶる「**元服**（烏帽子着祝い）」や、女子が初めて鉄漿をつける「鉄漿付け祝い」も行なわれていました。

⑨成人の日は、こうした伝統的な成人になるための儀式を地方自治体が成人式として全国一斉に行なうために、1947(昭和23)年から国が定めたものです。

神道式の結婚式

Shinto-style Wedding

三献の儀
The 3x3 Exchange of Ceremonial Cups

神さまに結婚の誓い
を述べます。

The couple take a
marriage vow in
front of the god.

誓詞奏上
The Marriage Vow

3つの盃で、新郎新
婦が交互にお酒を飲
みます。

The couple take
turns drinking *sake*
from three cups.

玉串奉奠
Offering a Branch of a Holy Tree

二人で、玉串を神殿に
ささげます

The bride and bride-
groom offer a branch
of a holy tree togeth-
er.

お宮参り

Baby's First Visit to a Shrine

お宮参りに行くときは、父方の
祖母が赤ちゃんを抱きます。

On the way to the shrine, the
baby is held by the grandmother
on the father's side.

84

お食い初めの膳

The Small Table for a Baby's First Food

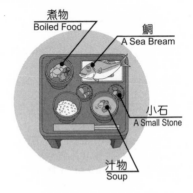

煮物
Boiled Food

鯛
A Sea Bream

小石
A Small Stone

汁物
Soup

生後100日ごろに、祝い膳を用意して、赤ちゃんの成長を祝います。

At around 100 days after birth, the family sets a small table for a meal to celebrate the baby's growth.

七五三

Festival for Children Aged Seven, Five, and Three

七五三には、千歳飴を食べて祝います。千歳飴は直径1センチくらいの細長い飴で、鶴・亀など、縁起のいい図案が描かれた、細長い袋に入っています。

At this festival, children aged seven, five, and three celebrate with a Thousand-year Candy. This candy is long and thin, one centimeter in diameter, and placed in a long, thin bag with a picture of a crane and a turtle on it.

千歳飴
The Thousand-year Candy

34. Funerals and Religion

①The Japanese people believe in many different religions
　　　　　　　　　　　　　～を信仰する　　　　　　　　　　　　　　宗教
such as *Shinto*, Buddhism, and Christianity. ②It is true that
たとえば～　神道　　仏教　　　　キリスト教　　　　　　確かに～だが―
there are many believers of each religion but most people
　　　　　　　　信者
don't always follow the traditions of their religion. ③ Quite
いつも～するわけではない　～に従う　　　　　　　　　　　　　　かなり多くの人々
a few people make their first visit of the year to shrines on
　　　　　　　神社に初詣に行く
New Year's but call a Buddhist priest for Buddhist services
　　　　　　　　　　　　僧侶　　　　　　　　　法要
in the Bon Festival. ④There are believers of Buddhism who
　　お盆
call a *Shinto* priest to have a ceremony to purify the land
　　　　神主　　　　　　　　　　　　　　　土地を清めるために(→地鎮祭をするために)
before they build their house.

⑤Especially, as for Buddhism and *Shinto*, there are many
　　　　　　　　～に関していえば
people who believe in both religions. ⑥That is because
　　　　　　　　　　　　　　　　　　　　　　　それは～だからだ
Shingi-shinko,or pre-*Shinto* worship, took root in the life of
　　　　　　　　　　　　　　　　崇拝　　　　～に根ざしていた
the Japanese people before Buddhism was introduced into
　　　　　　　　　　　　　　　　　　　　　　　　　～に伝来した
Japan. ⑦The Japanese people accepted Buddhism without
　　　　　　　　　　　　　　　　　～を受け入れた
doing away with *Shinngi-shinko* when Buddhism was
～を捨てることなく
introduced in the sixth century. ⑧Therefore Buddhism and
　　　　　　6世紀に

Shinto beliefs exist together in Japan today.
　　　　信仰　　　存在する
⑨Funerals, except for Christians, are usually held in the
　葬式　　　　～を除いて　　キリスト教徒　　　　　　　　　　　　　　仏式で
Buddhist way in Japan. ⑩*Shinto* funerals are only seen

once in a while. ⑪The Japanese people have many
たまに　　　　　　　　　　　　　　　　　　　　　　　～のしきたりがたくさんある
traditions for sending off the dead and most of them come
　　　　　　　　死人を送る　　　　　　　　　　　　　　　　　～に由来する
from Buddhism.

---

34. 葬式と宗教

①日本には、**神道**、**仏教**、**キリスト教**をはじめとするさまざまな宗教があります。②それぞれの宗教の信者がいるわけですが、信者が厳密に自分の宗教のしきたりだけを守っているわけではありません。③正月に神社に初詣に行った人が、お盆には僧侶を呼んで先祖の法要を行なったりすることも、ごく一般的に行なわれています。④また、仏教徒でも家を建てるときに神社から神主さんを呼んで地鎮祭をするといったこともあります。

⑤特に仏教と神道に関しては、両方掛け持ちする信者が多くいます。⑥これは、仏教が伝来する以前から神祇信仰が日本人の生活に深く根ざしていたからです。⑦仏教は6世紀に日本に伝来しましたが、神祇信仰を捨てることなく仏教を取り込みました。⑧そのために、仏教と神道が混在することになったのです。

⑨さて、**葬式**ですが、日本では、葬式はキリスト教徒を除いて仏式で行なうことがほとんどです。⑩神道の葬式は稀にある程度です。⑪また、死人を送るためのさまざまなしきたりがありますが、そのほとんどは仏教に由来するものです。

35. The Last Drink

①When a person dies, the family at his or her <u>deathbed</u>
死の床
wets the person's <u>lips</u>. ②This ceremony is called *matsugo-*
~を湿らせる　唇
no-mizu or *shini-mizu*, the last drink.

③Some say that *matsugo-no-mizu* comes from a <u>historical</u>
故事
<u>event</u> written in a <u>Buddhist text</u> called *Jo-agon-kyo* which
仏教経典
<u>took place</u> when <u>Buddha</u> was dying.
起こった　　　釈迦
④Buddha, who was dying <u>by a river</u>, <u>felt thirsty</u> and <u>asked</u>
川のほとりで　喉の渇きを覚えた　~を求める
his <u>pupil</u>, Ananda, for some water. ⑤Ananda said that the
弟子
river water was <u>muddy</u> but Buddha asked him again and
にごった
again. ⑥Ananda <u>had no choice</u>, and went to the river again
仕方がなかった
to get some water. ⑦<u>This time</u>, he found that the river
今度は
water, which was not clear <u>a little while ago</u>, was <u>perfectly</u>
つい先ほどまで　　　澄みわたっていた
<u>clear</u>. ⑧He <u>scooped up</u> some water and <u>gave Buddha a</u>
~をすくい上げた　　　　　~に飲ませた
<u>drink</u>. ⑨From this historical event, the custom of giving

water to a dead person started.

⑩<u>Traditionally</u>, people <u>don't</u> give the dead person a drink
伝統的に　　　　　~せずに―する

but only wet his or her lips with a Japanese star anise or
chrysanthemum leaf. ⑪ In most cases today, however, dry
cotton is used instead of leaves.

アニス
しきみ
クリサンサマム
菊
葉
ほとんどの場合
脱脂綿
〜の代わりに

35. 末期の水

① 人が臨終を迎えると、付き添っている家族は口を湿らせます。
② この儀式は「末期の水」あるいは「死に水」といわれています。
③ 末期の水は『長阿含経』という経典にある、次のようなお
釈迦さまの死に際の故事に由来するという説があります。
④ 川のほとりで最期を迎えたお釈迦さまは喉の渇きを覚えて、
弟子の阿難に水を求めます。⑤ 川の水がにごっていたので、阿
難がお釈迦さまにそう告げましたが、お釈迦さまは水を求め続
けます。⑥ 仕方なく阿難は再び川に水を求めて行きました。⑦ す
ると，つい先ほどまでにごっていた川の水がきれいに澄みわた
っていました。⑧ 阿難はその水を汲んでお釈迦さまに飲ませま
した。⑨ この話から、臨終を迎えた人に水を与える習慣が生ま
れたといわれています。
⑩ 伝統的な方法では、しきみや菊の葉を水で濡らし、唇を湿ら
せる程度に与えます。⑪ しかし、最近は、ガーゼや水で湿らせ
た脱脂綿などを葉の代用として使うことが、ほとんどです。

36. The Last Bath after Death

①*Yukan*, having a last bath, is a ceremony where the dead
<u>最後の風呂に入ること</u>

receive a bath. ②Today many people die in a hospital, so
<u>受ける</u>

nurses wipe and clean their bodies with gauze and alcohol.
<u>～を拭く</u>　　　　　　　<u>ガーゼ</u>　　<u>アルコール</u>

③This is not *yukan*, however, but *seishiki*, in which people

wipe a dead body clean. ④To soak the dead body in a tub and
<u>～をきれいに拭く</u>　　　<u>～をたらいにつける</u>

wash it clean by the family is called *Yukan* in the true sense.
<u>～をきれいに洗う</u>　　　　　　　　　<u>本来の意味で</u>

⑤The dead are prepared to leave this world through *yukan*.
　　　　<u>～する準備ができて</u>　<u>この世を去る(→死ぬ)</u>

⑥The root of this ceremony is based on the idea that human
<u>根底</u>　　　　　　　　<u>～に基づいている</u>

beings come to this world when they are born and go to the
　　　　　　<u>この世</u>

other world when they die. ⑦When a baby is born, people
<u>あの世</u>

give it a first bath, wash it and wrap it in white cloth. ⑧On
<u>産湯</u>　　　　　　　<u>～を白い布でくるむ</u>

the other hand, a dead body is cleaned by *yukan* and

dressed in white. ⑨It is thought that these two ceremonies
<u>白装束を着せる</u>

at birth and at death make a pair because they have bathing
　　　　　　　　<u>対になる</u>　　　　　　<u>風呂に入ること</u>

in common.
<u>共通して</u>

⑩It is a tradition that people lower the water temperature of
<u>～するのがしきたりである</u>　　<u>水温を下げる</u>

ubu-yu, the first bath, by <u>adding cold water to</u> hot water, but
<u>　　　　　　　　　　　　　　</u>
〜に冷たい水を足すこと

<u>raise the water temperature</u> of *yukan*, the last bath, by
〜を上げる

<u>adding hot water to cold water</u>, called *sakasa-mizu*.
〜に湯を足すこと

36. 湯灌の儀

①「**湯灌**」というのは、遺体を沐浴させることです。②最近は病院で臨終を迎えることが多く、看護婦さんがアルコールやガーゼで体を拭いて、清めてくれます。③これは「清拭」であり、湯灌ではありません。④湯灌とは遺体をたらいにつけ、家族が洗い清めることです。

⑤湯灌は死者を送り出す準備です。⑥その根底にあるのは、人間は誕生によってこの世にやって来て、死によって別世界へ旅立って行くという考え方です。⑦赤ちゃんが生まれると、産湯につけて清めてから、白いおくるみで包みます。⑧一方、遺体は湯灌で清めてから白装束を着せます。⑨この二つの儀式は、この世に生まれたときと、この世から去っていくときに湯浴みするという意味で、対応していると考えられています。

⑩産湯の湯は、湯に水を足して温度を下げますが、湯灌の湯は「**逆さ水**」といって、水に湯を足して温度を上げてつくることになっています。

37. The Last Clothes

①After finishing *yukan*, the last bath, people shave a male's
男性の髭を剃る
face or put make-up on a female's face and then the body is
女性の顔に化粧する
dressed in *shini-shozoku*, or the last clothes. ②Japanese
最後の服(→死装束)
people think that the spirits of the dead go on a trip to the
霊　　　　　　　　　　　～へ旅立つ
land of the dead so the last clothes they wear are similar to
冥土　　　　　　　　　　　　　　　　　　　　　　　～と同じ
traditional Japanese traveling clothes. ③Typical clothes for
旅の服装　　　　　　　　　　　典型的な
the dead are a white *kimono*, coverings for the back of the
手甲
hands, leggings, and a cloth wallet hung from the neck. ④It
脚絆　　　　　　頭陀袋　　　　首から下げられた
is a tradition to put a six *mon* coin in the wallet. ⑤It is said
～するのがしきたりである 六文銭　　　　　　　　　　　　～といわれている
that this coin will be used to pay for crossing the *sanzu*
三途の川を渡るために
river, which runs between this world and the other world.
この世　　　　　　あの世
⑥A triangular white cloth is put on the forehead of the
三角形の　　　　　　　　　　　　　　　　額に
dead.

⑦This white *kimono* is called *kyo-katabira*, winding sheet
死者を包む布
with Buddhist texts written on its white background. ⑧It is
経文　　　　　　　　　　　白地に
thought that these Buddhist texts wash away all sins the
洗い流す

92

dead committed in this world and let them go to Heaven.
死者がこの世で犯した罪　　　　　　　　　　　　　天国

⑨It is a tradition to dress the body in this white *kimono*

with the left side under the right.
左前に

⑩These days, however, not many people dress the dead in

white. ⑪Instead, they dress them in the clothes they liked

before they died. (see p.110)

---

37. 死装束

①湯灌を終えた遺体は、男性なら髭を剃り、女性は化粧をさせて**死装束**を着せます。②人間の霊は死後、冥土へ旅立つと考えられているため、死装束は日本の伝統的な旅の服装に近いものです。③その典型的なものは、白い着物に**手甲・脚絆**をつけ、**頭陀袋**をかけたいでたちです。④頭陀袋の中には**六文銭**を入れることになっています。⑤これは**三途の川**の**渡し賃**といわれています。⑥頭には三角形の白い布をつけます。

⑦白い着物は**経帷子**と呼ばれるもので、白地に経文が書かれたものです。⑧この経文により、生前の罪が滅せられ、**極楽往生**できると考えられていました。⑨この白い着物は、通常とは逆に**左前**に着せることになっています。

⑩最近は、遺体に白装束を着せることは少なくなりました。⑪そのかわりに、生前、気に入っていた服装で送るようになりました。

38. The Pillow Decoration

①When a person dies, the Japanese lay the person with his
〜を北枕に寝かせる

or her head to the north, and put out a *makura-kazari*, a
〜を飾る

pillow decoration, by the bedside. ②*Makura-kazari* is a
枕飾り　　　　　枕元に

kind of altar. ③People put rice, water, a bell, an incense
祭壇　　　　　〜の上に置く　　鈴　　香炉

burner, rice dumplings, lighted candles, a plant named
団子　　　　　火を燈したロウソク

Japanese star anise in a vase, and such on a small table
しきみという植物を立てた花瓶　　〜など　　白木の台

made of plain wood or on a tray.
お盆

④The Japanese people believe that the dead start on a trip
〜へ旅立つ

to the land of the dead or the other world. ⑤The *Sanzu* river
冥土　　　　　　あの世　　　　　三途の川

is on the way to that place. ⑥Those who cross it safely can
あの世　　　〜する人　　〜を無事に渡る

get to the land of the dead, but those who are washed away
〜に着く　　　　　　　　　　　　　〜に流される

by the river go to Hell. ⑦People think that the dead eat rice
地獄

and rice dumplings before their trip and the candles are to

light up their dark way. ⑧The Japanese star anise is a tree
〜を照らす　　暗い道

which has a unique smell. ⑨It is said that it protects the
独特の香り　　　　　　　　　　　〜を—から守る

spirits of the dead against evil spirits.
霊　　　　　　　　悪霊

⑩It was a custom to put out the pillow decoration until the
~する習慣があった

day the dead would be placed in a coffin. ⑪However,
遺体が納棺される日

because most people die in a hospital these days, the pillow

decoration is rarely seen. (see p.110)
ほとんど～ない

---

38. 枕飾り

①人が死ぬと北枕に寝かせ、枕元に「**枕飾り**」を用意します。
②枕飾りというのは、一種の祭壇です。③白木の台やお盆など
を用意して、その上に、枕飯、水、鈴、香炉、枕団子、火を
燈したロウソク、しきみという植物を1本立てた花瓶などを
並べます。
④人が死ぬと、死者の霊は冥土、すなわち死後の世界に旅立つ
と考えられてきました。⑤旅の途中には、三途の川があります。
⑥これを無事に渡ると、冥土にたどり着きますが、途中で川に
流されると地獄に落ちてしまいます。
⑦枕飯や枕団子は、その旅に出るための腹ごしらえ、ロウソク
の明かりは、暗い道を旅するための明かりです。⑧しきみは、
独特の香りがある木です。⑨旅の途中、死者の霊を悪霊から守っ
てくれるとされています。
⑩枕飾りは、遺体を納棺するまで飾っておくことになっていま
した。⑪しかし、病院で死ぬことが圧倒的に多くなった近年、「枕
飾り」はほとんど見られなくなりました。

39. The Opposite Way

①In Japan, it is a custom to do the opposite to the dead
　　　　　　　　～する習慣がある　　　～に―とは逆さまのことをする　死者
from what the living usually do in their daily life. ②This
　　　　　　生者
was called *sakasa-goto*, the opposite way. ③A well-known
　　　　　　　　　　逆さごと
example of this is when Japanese people dress the dead
　　　　　　　　　　　　　　　　　　　　　　　　～に服を着せる
hidari-mae, the left side of the *kimono* placed under the
　　　　　　　着物の左側を右側の下に置いて
right, which is opposite to that of the living. ④In addition
　　　　　　　　　　　　　　　　　生きている人　　それに加えて
to that, there are many rules of *sakasa-goto*.

⑤*Sakasa-mizu*, the opposite water, is made by adding
　　　　　　　　　　　　　　　　　　　　　～を―に加えることによって作られる
boiling water to cold for *yukan*, the last bath. ⑥In everyday

life, people usually make warm water by adding cold water

to hot but *sakasa-mizu* is done in the opposite way.
　　　　　　　　　　　　　　　　　　　　　逆のやり方で
⑦People also put the *kimono* or *futon*, a Japanese-style
　　　　　　　　　　　　　　　　　　　　　　　日本式の寝具
bedding, on the dead upside down, which is called *sakasa-*
　　　　　　　　　　　　上下逆さまに
kimono.

⑧There are some ideas as to why these customs of *sakasa-*
　　　　　　　　～についてのいくつかの説
goto were started.

⑨The first idea is that people do the opposite to the dead

because, in the other world, everything is opposite from
〜なので　　　あの世では

this world. ⑩The second idea is that people do the opposite
この世

to the dead to draw a line between death and life. ⑪Some
　　　　　　　　〜のあいだに境界線をひく

say *sakasa-goto* is done to keep off evil.
　　　　　　　　　　　　　　　　魔よけする

---

39. 逆さごと

①日本では、死者に対して日常と逆さまのことをする習慣があります。②それは「逆さごと」と呼ばれていました。③よく知られている例が、死者に着物を着せるとき、通常とは逆に、左側が内側になるように合わせる「左前」です。④ほかにも、「逆さごと」の決まりは、多く見られます。

⑤湯灌には、水に熱湯を加えて熱くした「逆さ水」を使います。⑥日常、ぬるま湯をつくるときは、熱湯を水で薄めますが、「逆さ水」は逆のつくり方です。⑦遺体に着物や布団をかけるときは、上下逆さまにかけ、「逆さ着物」とします。

⑧このような「逆さごと」の習慣が生まれた理由については、いくつかの説があります。

⑨第一に、死後の世界はすべて逆になっていると考えられていて、それにあわせるためにすべてを逆さまにするという説です。⑩二番目は、死を日常から隔てるために、死者の身のまわりを日常と逆さまにするという説です。⑪また、魔よけの意味があるともいわれています。

40. Buddhist Name and Buddhist Tablet

①In Buddhism, Buddhist names are given to the dead. ②A
　仏教では　　　　仏教の名前(→戒名)
Buddhist name was originally given to a person who
　　　　　　　　　　　もともと
became a monk in order to show that they would live away
出家して僧になる　～するために　　　　　　　俗世間を離れて暮らす
from this world and practice strict Buddhism as a pupil of
　　　　　　　　厳しい仏教の教えを実践する(→修行する)　～の弟子として
Buddha.

③The dead also started receiving Buddhist names because

it was thought they went to the other world, practiced strict
　　　　　　　　　　　　　　あの世
Buddhism, and then became a Buddha there.
　　　　　　　　　　　仏陀になった(→往生した)
④A Buddhist tablet is a wooden tablet on which their
　位牌　　　　　　　　　木製の
Buddhist name is written. ⑤It is a custom to put it in a

Buddhist altar or keep it at the family temple after the
仏壇　　　　　　　　　　　　　　菩薩寺
funeral.
葬儀
⑥It is a Buddhist tradition to make a Buddhist tablet after
　～するのは仏教のしきたりである
death. ⑦This was introduced from China through the *Zen*
　　　　　　　　～から伝えられた　　　　　　　　　禅宗
sect and Sung studies. ⑧Some say the Buddhist tablet
　　　　　　宋学
comes from the *Shinto tama-shiro* and others say it comes

from the Confucian *i-ban*. ⑨*Tama-shiro* is a piece of wood
　　　　儒教の　　　　　　　　　　　　　　　　　　　木片
which a spirit is in. ⑩*I-ban* is also a piece of wood on
　　　　　霊
which the name of the dead is written and is used to

worship ancestors. ⑪Still others think these two customs
先祖を祀る　　　　　　　　　さらに～する人もいる
came together to become the Buddhist tablet.
一緒になった

---

40. 戒名と位牌

①仏教では、死者に**戒名**という名前をつけます。②戒名は、もともとは出家する僧侶に、俗世間を離れ、仏の弟子として修行することの証しとして与えられた名前です。

③これが死者にもつけられるようになったのは、人間は死ぬとあの世へ行き、仏の弟子として修行をし、往生すると考えられていたからです。

④**位牌**というのは、戒名が書かれた小さな木製の牌です。⑤葬儀の後は仏壇に納めたり、菩提寺に預けておくことになっています。

⑥人の死後、位牌をつくるのは仏教のしきたりです。⑦それは、禅宗と宋学とともに、中国から伝えられたものです。⑧その起源については、神道の霊代と儒教の位版に求める説があります。⑨霊代とは、霊魂が乗り移って宿る木片です。⑩位版とは、故人の名前を書いた木片で、先祖を祀るときに用いるものです。⑪これらが融合して位牌になったと考えられています。

41. Mourning Clothes

①The Japanese people started to wear black as *mo-fuku*, mourning clothes, in the *Taisho* periods. ②Before that, the relatives of the dead person wore white *ko-sode*, a short-sleeved *kimono* made of raw linen, raw cotton, or other bleached material, and it was worn with the left side under the right.

③By wearing the same color as the dead person's *shini-shozoku*, or last clothes, they showed they were relatives of the dead person. ④A dead person and their relatives were thought to be unclean. ⑤Therefore the dead person and his or her relatives dressed in white and gathered together apart from others for fear of passing this uncleanness to them. ⑥People came to dress in Western style clothes in the *Meiji* period. ⑦The Japanese government encouraged people to wear black Western clothes and a mourning band like Westerners when they were at a state funeral. ⑧As a result,

people came to think of black clothes as mourning clothes.
〜を─とみなす

⑨However, it was only after the World War II that people
第二次世界大戦

all around the country wore black Western clothes at
各地で

funerals.

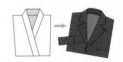

41. 喪服

①喪服の色が黒くなったのは、大正期以降のことです。②それ以前は血縁者の喪服は白で、麻や木綿の素地、または晒した白布で仕立てた小袖を左前に着用することになっていました。③これには、死装束と同じ色の白い喪服を着ることにより、死者の身内であるということを表わす意味がありました。④死者とその親族には、「けがれ」があると考えられていました。⑤それを周囲の人々に移さないように、死者と親族が同じ服装をしてかたまっていることになっていたのです。

⑥明治時代になって洋装するようになりました。⑦それにともない、政府は、国葬に参列する際には外国にならって喪章をつけ、黒い洋服を着用することを奨励しました。⑧その結果、黒い服が喪服として認知されました。⑨しかしながら、全国的に普及したのは昭和も戦後になってからです。

42. Wakes

①*Tsu-ya*, a wake, is a traditional event where relatives and
通夜　　　　　伝統的な行事　　　　　　　　親戚
friends of the dead person stay awake with him or her all
　　　　　　　　　　　　　一晩中起きている
through the night before the funeral.

②The wake is usually held in a simple way these days.
　　　　　　ふつうに行なわれる　簡略化された方法で
③Such simple *tsu-ya* are called *han-tsu-ya*, or a semi-wake.

④*Han-tsu-ya*, at which people eat, drink, and talk to each

other after a priest reads a Buddhist text, usually only go
　　　　　　僧侶　　お経をあげる　　　　　　　　　　続く
on for two hours. ⑤However, at the traditional *tsu-ya*,

people stay with the dead person keeping the incense sticks
　　　　　　　　　　　　　　　線香と灯明をつけたまま
lit and the room lighted until morning.

⑥Some say that *tsu-ya* comes from *mogari*, which was held
　　　　　　　　　　　　　～に由来する　　　　　　行なわれた
in Japan in the old days. ⑦*Mogari* was a ceremony, in
　　　　　　　　　　　　　　　　　　　　　　　　儀式
which people spent days with a dead body praying for it to
　　　　　　　　祈りながら過ごした
come to life again. ⑧In the end, after seeing the body rot
再び生き返る　　　　　最後に　　　　遺体が朽ちるのを見ること
down, they sadly accepted the death and said goodbye.
　　　　　　　死を受け入れた
⑨Others say that *tsu-ya* comes from a historical event
　　　　　　　　　　　　　　　　　　　　　　　　故事

102

which took place after Buddha died. ⑩It is said that

Buddha's pupils, who mourned their teacher's death, talked
　　　　　　　　　　～を悼んだ　　　　　師の死
about his teachings all through the night. ⑪For this reason,
　　　教え
many think that this is the origin of *tsu-ya*.
　　　　　　　　　　　起源

⑫Today, people tend to make more of the *tsu-ya* than of the
　　　　　　　　　～する傾向にある　～を―より重視する
funeral.

---

42. 通夜

①通夜とは、葬儀の前の晩に故人の親戚や親しかった人々が、遺体とともに一夜を過ごす、しきたりです。

②現在は簡略化した形をとることが多くなっています。③簡略化した通夜は半通夜などといわれます。④そこでは、僧侶がお経をあげたあと、集まった人が酒を酌み交わしながら会食して、２時間くらいで終わってしまいます。⑤しかし、朝まで線香や灯明を絶やさず、遺体に付き添うのが本来の通夜です。

⑥通夜の起源は、日本で古来から行なわれていた「殯」にあるという説があります。⑦殯とは、遺体とともに過ごしながら、その蘇生を願う儀式でした。⑧そして、やがて朽ちていく遺体を見ながら別れを惜しみ、死を確認するのです。

⑨もう一つの説は、お釈迦さまが入滅したときの故事にならったものとする説です。⑩お釈迦さまの入滅後、死を悼む弟子たちはお釈迦さまの教えを夜通し語り合ったと伝えられています。⑪これが通夜の起源になったというものです。

⑫現在は、通夜が葬式の代わりに重視される傾向があります。

43. Funerals

①When Japanese people are at a funeral, they always give
　　　　　　　　　葬式に参列する　　　　　　　必ず〜する
some money in an envelope to a receptionist as a *ko-den*, or
　　　　　　　　封筒　　　　　　受付人
funeral offering. ②In the old days, it was a custom to bring
葬式のお供え　　　　　　　　　　　　　　　　　　　〜を〜に持っていく
some food for the family which gave the funeral. ③Later
　　　　　　　　　　　　　葬式を出した　　　　　　　のちに
on, people came to bring money instead of food, and this is
　　　　〜を持っていくようになった　　　〜の代わりに
believed to be the origin of *ko-den* today.
　　　　　　　　　起源

④Buddhist-style funerals are the most common in Japan.
仏教式の葬式
⑤In this style, people at the funeral burn incense for the
　　　　　　　　　　　　　　　　　焼香をする
dead person one after another while a priest reads a
　　　　　　　一人ずつ　　　　〜するあいだ　僧侶　　お経をあげる
Buddhist text. ⑥The immediate family is the first to burn
　　　　　　　　　　最も近い家族
incense followed by relatives in order of closest blood
　　　　〜が続いて(焼香する)　親戚　　血縁の濃い順に
relation. ⑦Finally, friends, in order of closest relationship
　　　　　　　　　　　　　　故人と関係が近い順に
to the dead, burn incense last. ⑧*Sho-ko* is as important a
　　　　　　　　　　　　　　　　　　　　〜と同じくらい重要である
custom for people at Buddhist funerals as flower offerings
　　　　　　　　　　　　　　　　　　　　　　　　　献花
are at Christian-style funerals.
　　　キリスト教式の葬式
⑨After all the people finish *sho-ko* and the priest finishes
最後に

the Buddhist text, they say goodbye to the dead person <u>for</u>

<u>the last time</u> and he or she is taken to <u>a place to burn the</u>
最後に　　　　　　　　　　　　　　　　　　遺体を灰にする場所(→火葬場)

<u>body to ashes.</u> ⑩Only relatives and <u>close</u> friends go there
　　　　　　　　　　　　　　　　　　　親しい

with the dead person.

43. 葬儀

①葬式に参列するときは、必ず「**香典**」としてお金を包み、受付で渡すことになっています。②もともと、葬儀の期間中に食べ物を喪家に持参する習慣がありました。③これらがお金に形を変え、現在のような香典になったと考えられています。

④日本でもっとも一般的な葬式は仏教式です。⑤僧侶がお経をあげるなか、参列する人たちが一人ずつ**焼香**します。⑥焼香の順序は、まず喪主が一番最初で次に血縁の濃い順です。⑦そして、間柄が近い順に行なうことになっています。⑧焼香は、キリスト教の葬式の献花のように、葬式の参列者にとって一番大切な儀式です。

⑨参列者全員が焼香をすませ、僧侶が読経を終えると、全員が遺体に最後の別れを告げ、遺体を火葬場に送り出します。⑩火葬場には、親族とごく身近な友人だけが付き添っていきます。

44. Buddhism and Incense

①In Japanese Buddhism, people almost always burn
<u>incense</u> when they <u>pray to</u> the dead or Buddha. ②This is
香をたく   ～を拝む
called *sho-ko.* ③There are two kinds of incense: <u>incense</u>
<u>sticks</u> and <u>incense powder.</u> ④Incense powder is what people
線香   抹香
use at <u>funerals</u> and <u>wakes.</u>
葬儀   通夜
⑤To do *sho-ko,* you pick up <u>a pinch of</u> incense powder,
～するために   ひとつまみ
<u>scatter</u> it on <u>a charcoal fire</u> and let it burn. ⑥Sometimes,
～をパラパラと落とす   炭火
people repeat this a few times but <u>the number of times</u> and
回数
<u>how it is done</u> <u>depend on</u> the Buddhist <u>sect.</u> ⑦When people
それがどのようになされるか   ～による   宗派
do it three times, they <u>are respecting</u> <u>the three treasures</u> in
敬っている   三宝
Buddhism, which are the <u>Buddha,</u> <u>Buddhist texts,</u> and
仏   経典
<u>Buddhist priests.</u> ⑧This <u>removes</u> the three poisons of
僧   ～を取り除く   三毒
<u>desire,</u> <u>anger,</u> and <u>illusion.</u>
欲望   怒り   迷い
⑨People must <u>keep the fire of</u> incense <u>from going out</u> for a
～の火を絶やさない
while after the funeral. ⑩It is said that the spirits of the
dead <u>take a forty-nine-days trip from</u> this world to the other
～から―を49日間旅をする

world and they are <u>judged</u> during this trip. ⑪These 49 days
裁きを受ける
are called *chu-in*, the period between life and death.
⑫People keep the fire of incense burning for forty-nine
days because they believe that incense <u>protects</u> the spirits
〜を守る
of the dead during *chu-in*. (see p.111)

---

44. 仏教と香

①日本の仏教では、死者や仏さまを拝むときには、必ずといっていいほど、**香**をたきます。②これを**焼香**といいます。③香には細い棒状の線香と粉状の抹香があります。④葬式や通夜で使うのは抹香です。

⑤焼香の方法ですが、抹香を少量、指でつまんで炭火の上にパラパラと落として焚きます。⑥これを2、3回繰り返すこともありますが、その回数と方法は、仏教の宗派により異なります。⑦3回行なう場合には、仏教の三宝である「仏・法・僧」を敬っているのです。⑧これは、三毒である「貪（欲望）・瞋（怒り）・癡（心の迷い）」を滅することを意味するとされています。

⑨香は、葬式が終わっても、しばらくのあいだ絶やしてはいけないといわれています。⑩死者の霊は死後49日間、現世から来世に旅しながら裁きを受けるとされています。⑪この期間は**中陰**と呼ばれています。⑫49日間、香を絶やさないようにするのは、中陰のあいだ、香が死者の霊を守っていると信じられているからです。

45. Buddhist Services for the Dead

①The dead go on a trip between life and death for forty-nine
死者　　旅をする　　　　　　　生と死
days during *chu-in*. ②It is thought that the dead are judged
　　　　　　　　　　　　　　　　　　　　　　　　　　　　　　　　　　　　　　　～に対する裁きを受ける
for what they did in this world during this trip. ③The last
　　　　　　　　　　　　この世
judgment of *Enma-dai-o*, the king of Hell, is made on the
最後の裁きが下される　　　　　　　　地獄の王
forty-ninth day, the final day of the trip. ④At this judgment,

the king of Hell decides which of six worlds, from Hell to
　　　　　　　　　決める　　～のうちのどれか
Heaven, the dead will be born again in. ⑤Because the first
　　　　　　　　　　　　　　生まれ変わる
judgment on the seventh day and the last judgment on the

forty-ninth day are especially important, the family holds a

special service for the dead on these days. ⑥*Sho-nano-ka* is
特別な供養
the Buddhist service for the dead on the seventh day after
　　　　死者に対する法要
death and *shiju-ku-nichi* is the service on the forty-ninth day.

⑦Family members are thought to be unclean until the forty-ninth
　　　　　　　　　　　　　　　　　　　　　　　　　　けがれている
day. ⑧During this period, they are in mourning, which is called
　　　　　　　　　　　　　　　　　喪に服している
mo-chu or *ki-chu*, so they must not take part in happy events.
　　　　　　　　　　　　　　　　　　　　　　　　　　　　　　　祝い事
⑨The forty-ninth day after death is not only the day of the
　　　　　　　　　　　　　　　　　　　～だけではなく―でもある

last judgment but also the day when *ki-chu* is over. ⑩After
終わる

the family holds a service for the dead where a priest reads
僧侶

a Buddhist text, the family treats people at the service to a
お経をあげる　　　　　　　　　　～に—をごちそうする

meal of fish and drinks. ⑪This party is called *shojin-otoshi*,

or coming out of mourning. ⑫The family can go back to
喪が明けること

their normal lifestyle after it ends.

---

45. 死者に対する法要

①死者は、49 日間かけて中陰を旅をします。②この間、7 日ごとに生前の行ないに対する裁きを受けるとされています。③そして、閻魔大王による最後の裁きを受けるのが、旅の最終日にあたる 49 日目です。④この判決により、地獄から天国まで 6 段階ある世界のどこに生まれ変わるかが決まるのです。⑤特に、最初の裁きである 7 日目と最後の裁きである 49 日目が重要なことから、遺族はこの日に念入りに供養を行ないます。⑥これが初七日と 49 日の法要です。

⑦一方、遺族も 49 日までは死のけがれに染まっていると考えられています。⑧この期間を喪中あるいは忌中といい、祝い事に参加してはいけないことになっています。

⑨49 日は、死者が最後の裁きを受ける日であると同時に、忌中が明ける日です。⑩僧侶にお経をあげてもらって死者を供養したあとで、参列者を魚料理や酒でもてなします。⑪これを「精進落とし」と呼びます。⑫これを終えると、遺族は平常の生活に戻ることになります。

死装束
The Last Clothes

冥土へ旅立つための衣装である死装束は、日本の伝統的な旅の服装に近いものです。

The last clothes, used to dress the dead at a funeral, are for going on a trip to the land of the dead so they are similar to traditional Japanese clothes for a trip.

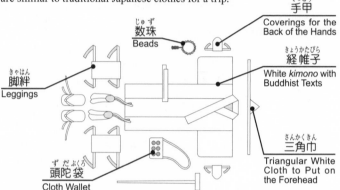

数珠
Beads

手甲
Coverings for the Back of the Hands

脚絆
Leggings

経帷子
White *kimono* with Buddhist Texts

頭陀袋
Cloth Wallet

三角巾
Triangular White Cloth to Put on the Forehead

枕飾り
The Pillow Decoration

枕飾りは、死後の世界に行くまでの旅の装備を枕元に置いたものです。

The pillow decoration is made up of the dead person's belongings for the trip to the land of the dead.

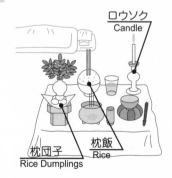

ロウソク
Candle

枕団子
Rice Dumplings

枕飯
Rice

葬儀の焼香

Burning Incense at a Funeral

①遺族と僧侶に礼をします。

Bow to the family of the dead person and the priest.

②祭壇に一礼して合掌し、抹香をつまみ目の高さにおしいただきます（浄土真宗を除く）。

Bow once to the altar, join your hands together, pick up a pinch of incense powder with one hand, and lift it to your eye level. (It is not the case of the Jodo-shin sect)

③抹香を香炉に落とします。

Scatter it on the incense burner.

④再び合掌し、一礼します。

Join your hands together and bow once again.

The Twenty-four Solar Terms/ 二十四節気

The 24 Solar Terms were made to correct the out-of-sync with the seasons caused by the lunar calendar and to divide a year into four seasons in the civil war period in China. A year was divided into 12 *chuki* and 12 *sekki*. Each of them was placed one after the other and was given name describing its own season.

二十四節気は、中国の戦国時代に太陰暦による季節のずれを補正し、春夏秋冬の四季に分けるために考えられました。1年を12の「中気」と12の「節気」に分けて交互に配置し、季節を表わす名前がつけられています。

名称	新暦の目安	意味	
立春	2月4日	春が始まる日。節分の翌日	spring
雨水	2月18〜19日	雪が融けて雨が降り出す頃	
啓蟄	3月5〜6日	土中にいた虫が地上に這い出す頃	
春分	3月20〜21日	春の彼岸の中日で、昼夜の長さがほぼ等しくなる日	
清明	4月4〜5日	清らかで明るい季節の頃	
穀雨	4月20〜21日	春雨が降って、穀物を成長させる頃	
立夏	5月5〜6日	夏が始まる日	summer
小満	5月21日	万物が充満し、草木枝葉が繁る頃	
芒種	6月5〜6日	麦などの芒（穀類の堅い毛）のある穀物の種をまく頃	
夏至	6月21〜22日	昼が最も長く、夜が最も短くなる日	
小暑	7月7〜8日	暑さが厳しくなる頃	
大暑	7月22〜23日	暑さが最高になる日	
立秋	8月7〜8日	秋の始まる日	fall
処暑	8月23〜24日	暑さが終わり、涼風が吹く頃	
白露	9月7〜8日	野草に露が宿る頃	
秋分	9月23日	秋の彼岸の中日で、昼夜の長さがほぼ等しくなる日	
寒露	10月8〜9日	寒気で露が凍る頃	
霜降	10月23〜24日	霜が降り、冬が近づく頃	
立冬	11月7〜8日	冬が始まる日	winter
小雪	11月22〜23日	初雪が降り始める頃	
大雪	12月7〜8日	雪が多くなる頃	
冬至	12月21〜22日	夜が最も長く、昼が最も短くなる日	
小寒	1月5〜6日	寒風や降雪が激しくなる頃。寒の入り	
大寒	1月20〜21日	寒さが最高になる日	

Chapter 3

Traditions in Daily Life

第3章

暮らしのしきたり

46. Japanese Clothing

①It is said that the *ko-sode*, a short-sleeved *kimono* which
短い袖の着物(→小袖)

was worn as underwear until the end of the *Heian* period,
下着として

has evolved into the traditional Japanese *kimonos* of today.
〜に進化してきた

②In the Middle Ages, the *ko-sode* began to be worn as
中世に

outer clothing and later became what the *kimono* is today.
上着として   現在の着物

③It is too bad that the *kimono*, which has such a long
〜はとても残念である

history, is not seen so often now. ④Mothers used to go to
それほど見られない   〜したものだった

their children's entrance and graduation ceremonies in
入学式や卒業式

kimonos until about 30 years ago but very few mothers do

so now. ⑤Nowadays, you only see women in *furi-sode*,
〜を着た女性

long-sleeved *kimonos*, at university graduation ceremonies,
長い袖の着物(→振袖)

coming-of-age ceremonies, or wedding dinners.
成人式   披露宴

⑥Even today, many Japanese women long to wear
〜するのに憧れる

brilliantly colored *kimonos*. ⑦However, they don't wear
艶やかな色の

them very often because these *kimonos* are difficult to put

on and wear properly. ⑧A *kimono* has no buttons so
きちんと   ボタン

women have to put it on by tying many strings. ⑨Today,
　　　　　　　 <u>それを着る</u>　<u>多くの紐で結ぶことによって</u>

very few women can put on a *kimono* by themselves. ⑩ <u>In</u>
　　　　　　　　　　　　　　　　　 <u>自力で</u>

<u>many cases</u>, they <u>ask</u> a professional *kimono* <u>dresser</u> to do
<u>多くの場合</u>　　　　 <u>頼む</u>　　　　　　　　　 <u>着付け師</u>

this for them. (see pp.122-123)
　<u>～のかわりに</u>

---

46. 和装

---

①現在、日本を代表する衣装である**着物**は、平安時代の末期まで下着として着用されていた**小袖**が形を変えたものだといわれています。②これが中世になると上着になり、やがて現在に見られる着物になりました。

③こんなに長い歴史を持つ着物ですが、残念なことに最近はあまり多くは見かけません。④30年ほど前までは、子供の入学式や卒業式に着物を着て行くお母さんが多かったのですが、これもほとんどいなくなってしまいました。⑤最近は大学の卒業式、成人式や友達の結婚式のために**振袖**を着ている女性を見かけるくらいです。

⑥今でも、艶やかな着物は多くの日本女性の憧れの的です。⑦にもかかわらず、着物を着ることが少なくなっているのは、美しく着るのが難しいからです。⑧着物には、ボタンのようなものがないので、何本もの紐で結んでいきます。⑨これを自分でできる人はあまりいません。⑩ほとんどの場合、専門家に**着付け**を頼んで、着せてもらいます。

47. The Kimono

①There are many kinds of *kimono*, and women choose one according to their age, the place they will visit, and so on.
~に応じて

②A woman's ceremonial dress is called a *tome-sode*, or
礼装

formal *kimono*. ③It has family emblems on it and has some
正式な　　　　　家紋

patterns around the bottom of it. ④The *kuro-tome-sode* is a
模様　　　　~の下

black formal *kimono* for married women. ⑤The *kuro-tome-*
既婚女性

sode is often worn by mothers at their children's weddings.
　　　　~によって着られる　　　　　　　　結婚式

⑥A *tome-sode* in colors other than black is called an *iro-*
黒以外の色の

tome-sode, or colored *tome-sode*, which are sometimes

worn by unmarried women.
未婚女性

⑦*Homon-gi*, or visiting *kimonos*, are formal dress for tea
正装

ceremony parties or other parties and are well-known for
茶会

their *eba* pattern. ⑧A *homon-gi* is sewn so that the pattern
絵羽模様　　　　~するように縫われる

continues unbroken throughout the *kimono*, and it is called an
途切れずに続く　　~のすみからすみまで

eba pattern. ⑨Some *homon-gi* have family emblems on them.

⑩Simple *homon-gi* are called *tsuke-sage* and have neither
~でも―でもない

an *eba* pattern nor family emblems. ⑪They fall in between
〜と—の中間にある

formal wear and casual wear.
普段着

⑫A *furi-sode* is a long-sleeved *kimono* which unmarried
長い袖の着物（→振袖）

women wear to wedding dinners and so on. ⑬It used to be a
披露宴

kimono for those who were under age but now is formal ceremonial
未成年者

dress for unmarried women like the *tome-sode* and *homon-gi.*

---

47. 着 物

①**着物**にもさまざまな種類があり、年齢や着て行く場所に応じたものを着ることになっています。

②女性の礼装とされているのが、**留袖**です。③家紋がついていて、裾に模様が入っています。④黒いものは、**黒留袖**といわれ、既婚女性の正装とされています。⑤子どもの結婚式に母親がよく着ているのが、黒留袖です。⑥黒以外の色の留袖は色留袖といわれ、未婚女性も着ることができます。

⑦**訪問着**は、茶会やパーティーなどに行くときに着る正装で、絵羽模様が特徴です。⑧絵羽模様とは、縫い目でつながるように描かれた柄です。⑨訪問着には、家紋を入れたものもあります。⑩訪問着を簡略化したものを**付け下げ**といい、絵羽模様がなく、家紋は付けません。⑪正装と普段着の中間です。

⑫**振袖**は、未婚の女性が結婚式などに着て行く、袖の長い着物です。⑬以前は振袖を着るのは未成年に限られていましたが、現在では未婚の女性の礼装として、留袖や訪問着に相当する格式のある着物です。

48. The Obi

①For Japanese-style clothing, an *obi*, or *kimono* sash, is
着物の帯
just as important as the *kimono*. ②This is because the color
これは～だからである　色の組み合わせ
coordination of the *obi* and *kimono* along with the choice of
～とともに　柄の選択
pattern according to the season show if the wearer has an
～に応じた　着る人
eye for beauty or not.
美的感覚がある
③There are many kinds of *obi* for women and most are 30
centimeters wide and four meters long. ④Women tie their
幅30センチ　　　　　長さ4メートル　　　　　～を帯で結ぶ
kimono with an *obi* by winding it around themselves many
巻くこと
times. ⑤The *fukuro-obi* is the most common among women
～のあいだでもっとも一般的である
today. ⑥It is a formal *obi* worn with the *tome-sode*, *furi-*
正式な
sode, and *homon-gi*.

⑦Until the *Taisho* period, women usually wore a *maru-obi*.

⑧A *maru-obi* is about 60 centimeters wide. ⑨Women fold
the width in half before putting it on. ⑩It is the most formal
幅半分に折る
obi but is only used by brides today.
花嫁
⑪There is also the *Nagoya-obi*, which is 60 centimeters

wide around the knot with the rest folded in half and sewn
結び目　　　　　　残りの部分　　　　　　　　縫われた

30 centimeters wide. ⑫The *Nagoya-obi*'s good point is that

it can be tied more freely than other *obis* but it is less formal
～より正式ではない

than a *fukuro-obi*, which is used for formal dress. ⑬In
正装

addition, there is the *han-haba-obi*, which is 15 centimeters
それに加えて

wide and worn with a *yukata*, a light summer *kimono*.
軽い夏の着物(→浴衣)

---

48. 帯

①和装で着物と同じくらい大切なのが**帯**です。②帯と着物の色の組み合わせや、季節感にあった柄を選ぶことが着る人のセンスの見せ所となるからです。

③女性用の帯にはいくつか種類がありますが、一般的なもので幅30センチ、長さは4メートルもあります。④これを何重にも巻いて締め、結びます。⑤現在、一番多く見られるのが、**袋帯**です。⑥袋帯は留袖、振袖、訪問着などと合わせて使われる正装用の帯です。⑦大正時代までは、**丸帯**が主流でした。⑧丸帯は幅60センチです。⑨これを幅半分に折って巻きます。⑩一番格式が高い帯ですが、現在は花嫁衣裳くらいにしか用いられません。

⑪結び目だけが幅60センチあり、ほかの部分は半分に折って30センチ幅に縫い合わせた**名古屋帯**などもあります。⑫比較的自由に結べることが特徴で、正装に用いる袋帯よりも格式が低いとされています。⑬そのほか、浴衣を着るときに用いる幅が15センチの**半幅帯**などがあります。

49. The Yukata

①Recently, the *yukata,* or light summer *kimono*, which was
<u>軽い夏の着物(→浴衣)</u>
originally worn when people took a bath, is <u>in fashion</u>
<u>おしゃれである</u>
again among young people.

②Before <u>the Modern Ages,</u> <u>very few</u> Japanese people had
<u>近世</u> <u>とても少ない</u>
the custom of bathing in a <u>bathtub.</u> ③Most of them cleaned
<u>湯船</u>
their bodies by <u>steam bath</u> or by <u>pouring</u> warm water <u>over</u>
<u>蒸し風呂</u> <u>～を―に浴びせる</u>
themselves. ④It was very hard to fill a bathtub with warm
water because they had to get the water from <u>wells</u> or <u>rivers</u>
<u>井戸</u> <u>川</u>
and <u>boil</u> it over a fire. ⑤People bathed in these ways <u>while</u>
<u>～を沸かす</u> <u>着ながら</u>
<u>wearing</u> a *yu-katabita*, which is thought to be <u>the original</u>
<u>原型</u>
<u>form</u> of *yukata.*

⑥When the bathtub became popular, people started taking
baths without clothes on and the *yu-katabira* was worn
after the bath. ⑦After the *Edo* period, the *yu-katabira* came
to be worn as summer clothes by many people and the
name was changed to *yukata.*

⑧Most of the *yukata* women wear today have colorful
色とりどりの模様

patterns but the traditional *yukata* were made from

materials dyed in indigo with undyed areas forming the
生地　　　藍で染められた　　　　染められていない部分

pattern. ⑨This style of dyeing is called *chugata-zome*, or

middle-style dyeing.(see p.122)

---

49. 浴衣

①最近は夏の若者のおしゃれ着として、再び注目されている
浴衣(ゆかた)ですが、古くは入浴の際に着用されていたものでした。
②近世以前は、現在のように湯船で入浴する習慣はほとんどあ
りませんでした。③蒸し風呂かお湯を浴びて体の汚れを落とし
ていたのです。④井戸や川から水を汲(く)んで、薪(まき)でお湯を沸(わ)かし
ていたため、湯船いっぱいに水を張って風呂を沸かすのは大変
な労力が必要だったからです。⑤そうした入浴の際に着用され
たのが、浴衣の原型と考えられている湯帷子(ゆかたびら)でした。
⑥やがて、湯船が普及し、裸で入浴する習慣が広まると、湯帷
子は入浴後の着物となりました。⑦江戸時代以降、これが夏衣
として広く愛用されるようになり、浴衣と呼ばれるようになり
ました。
⑧現代の女性が着る浴衣は、色とりどりの模様をあしらった
ものがほとんどですが、伝統的な浴衣は藍(あい)で模様を白く染め
抜いた生地で仕立てられたものです。⑨これは中形(ちゅうがた)染めと呼
ばれます。

振袖と留袖

The Long-sleeved Kimono and the Shortened Long-sleeved Kimono

振袖は未婚女性の第一礼装です。袖の丈が長いほどと格式が高いとされています。

A long-sleeved *kimono* is the most formal ceremonial dress for unmarried women. The longer the sleeves are the more formal the *kimono* is.

留袖には、「黒留袖」と「色留袖」があります。「黒留袖」は既婚女性の第一礼装です。

There are two kinds of shortened long-sleeved *kimono*: *kuro-tome-sode* and *iro-tome-sode*. *Kuro-tome-sode* is the most formal ceremonial dress worn by married women.

振袖
Furisode

留袖
Tomesode

浴衣

The Light Summer Kimono

浴衣は、本来は部屋着ですが、最近は夏のおしゃれ着として、若い人にも人気があります。

A light summer *kimono*, which was originally worn at home, is also popular and in fashion among young people today.

帯の結び方

How to Tie the Obi

太鼓結び
Drum Knot

ふだん着にも合う、代表的な女帯の結び方。

Typical knot for women's *obi* suited for casual *kimono*s, too.

文庫結び
Book-shaped Knot

浴衣の帯結びの基本形。振袖に使うこともある。

Basic knot for the light summer *kimono*. It is sometimes also used for the long-sleeved *kimono*.

貝の口
Shell's Mouth Knot

男女ともに使える、もっとも一般的な結び方。

The most common knot used for both men and women.

ふくらすずめ
Fat Sparrow Knot

振袖や訪問着に使われる結び方。

Knot for the long-sleeved *kimono* and the visiting *kimono*.

50. Rice

①Rice is the staple food of Japan. ②It has much to do with
　　　　　主食　　　　　　　　　　　　　　　　　　　　　～と関係がある
the Japanese way of living and their traditions.
　　　　　生活様式
③It is said that Southeast Asian rice plants were introduced
　　　　　　　　　東南アジアの稲
to Japan at the end of the *Jomon* period. ④After that, rice

became the main crop of Japan and, in growing rice, a new
　　　　　～の主要な農産物　　　　　　　稲作において
faith to gods such as the god of rice fields was born.
～に対する新しい信仰　　　　　　　　　　　　　生まれた
⑤Furthermore, the Japanese thought rice itself held the
　　さらに　　　　　　　　　　　　　　　　　　　　持った
power of the spirits. ⑥People today eat rice cakes, which
霊力　　　　　　　　　　　　　　　　　餅
are made of one type of rice, at happy events because
　　　　　　　　　　　　　　おめでたいときに
people in the old days thought they would get power from
　　　　　　　　　　　　　　　　　　　　　～から力を得る
the spirits by eating them. ⑦In the past, people believed in

many customs for getting both mental and physical power
　　　　　　　　　　　　　　精神的な　　　肉体的な
from rice. ⑧Some examples of these are *chikara-gome*, in

which people made mothers bite uncooked rice when they
　　　　　　～に噛ませた　　　　生米
gave birth to a baby, and *furi-gome*, in which people shook
～を産む　　　　　　　　　　　　　　　　　　　～を振った
a bamboo tube filled with rice by the bed of a patient in
米の入った竹筒　　　　　　　　　　　　　　　　　重病人

serious condition so that the patient could hear the sound.
 ~するように

⑨For such reasons, Japanese people today cannot do without
 ~なしですます

rice. ⑩However, it was not until the *Meiji* and *Taisho* period
 ~してはじめて―した

that it became their staple food. ⑪Before that, people usually

ate boiled cereal grains and vegetables or food mixed with a
 炊いた雑穀と野菜   少量の米を加えた食べ物

little rice because rice was very expensive.

---

50. 米

①米は日本人の主食です。②しかし、それだけでなく、さまざまな面で日本人の暮らしやしきたりと関わりをもっています。③東南アジア原産の稲が日本に渡来したのは、縄文時代の末期といわれています。④以後、稲は日本の主要な農作物となり、「田の神」といった稲作にまつわる信仰が生まれました。

⑤その一方で、米自身に霊力があるとも考えられてきました。⑥おめでたいときに餅米からつくった餅を食べるのは、それによって霊力を得られると考えられていたからです。⑦かつては、米から精神的、肉体的な力を得ようとするしきたりは、数多くありました。⑧出産のときに妊婦に生米を噛ませる「力米」、重病人の病床で竹筒に入れた米を振って音を聞かせる「振り米」などです。

⑨このように、米は日本人にはなくてはならないものです。⑩しかし、白米のご飯が主食となったのは、明治・大正時代以降と考えられています。⑪それ以前は米は高級品で、雑穀や野菜、あるいはそれらを米に混ぜ込んで炊いたものが庶民の主食でした。

51. Rice Steamed with Red Beans

① *Seki-han* is red-colored rice made by steaming sticky rice
赤い色をしたご飯　　　　　　　　蒸すことによって　餅米

with adzuki beans, black-eyed peas, and their stock.
小豆　　　　　　大角豆　　　　　　　　煮汁

② In Japan, *seki-han* became a food that symbolizes happy
〜を象徴する

events because people eat it when someone gets married or

a baby is born. ③ On the other hand, in some areas people

also eat it at funerals .

④ Some say that *seki-han* is made in the image of the red
〜をイメージして作られている　赤米

rice people used to grow in the old days. ⑤ Red rice is like
栽培する

plants that grow naturally in the wild and typically become
野生植物　　　　　　　　　　　　　　　典型的に

red as it grows.
成長するにつれて

⑥ It is polished and boiled to make rice whose color is red.
精米される

⑦ Still now, it is a custom to offer red rice to the gods at
〜を—に奉納する

some shrines.

⑧ It is thought that the custom of eating *seki-han* on happy

days was started because people thought red had the power

to keep off uncleanness. ⑨ Some people also eat *seki-han* at
〜を祓う　けがれ

funerals to ward off the uncleanness of death.
　　　　　～を祓う

51. 赤飯

①赤飯は、小豆や大角豆と、その煮汁を餅米に加えて蒸した、赤いご飯です。

②結婚や子どもの誕生など、おめでたいことがあったときに食べるので、日本では赤飯はおめでたい出来事を象徴する料理の一つとなっています。③その一方で、葬式のときにも食べる地域があります。

④赤飯の起源は、古来日本で栽培されていた赤米であるという説があります。⑤赤米は、野生種に近い品種で成長の過程で赤く色づくのが特徴です。

⑥これを精米して炊くと、赤いご飯になります。⑦いくつかの神社では、今でも赤米を奉納する習慣が残っています。

⑧めでたい日に赤飯を食べる習慣は、赤い色はけがれを祓う霊力があるとされたところから、生まれたと考えられています。
⑨葬式でも食べるのは、死のけがれを祓うという意味合いからです。

52. Salt

①Japan has neither rock salt nor lake salt so the Japanese people had to make salt from seawater. ②It takes much time and labor to make salt using this method. ③That is why people in the old days thought salt was important and holy. ④This led to the custom of offering salt to gods. ⑤People also believed salt had the power to wash away uncleanness. ⑥That is why people often poured seawater over themselves before they prayed to the god. ⑦Therefore they believed salt which was made from seawater had the same power. ⑧*Sumo* wrestlers throw salt into the *sumo* ring and people have used salt to purify various things such as their *Shinto* altar and old Japanese-style kitchen. ⑨People continue this custom of purifying with salt even today. ⑩It is a custom to throw salt in front of the door when people come back from funerals. ⑪They do this to wash away the uncleanness of death. ⑫A small mound of

salt is sometimes seen in front of restaurants in Japan.
⑬This means that the restaurant has already been purified

and is always <u>prepared to</u> purify <u>at any time.</u>
　　　　　　　～する準備ができている　　いつでも

---

52. 塩

①岩塩や湖塩がない日本では、**塩は海水からつくる必要**があ
りました。②海水から塩を得るためには、大変な手間がかかり
ます。③そのため、昔から塩は貴重なもの、神聖なものと考え
られました。④ここから、神さまへの供物として塩を供える習
慣が生まれました。

⑤また、塩には**けがれを清める力**があるとも考えられてきまし
た。⑥海水にも、もののけがれを清める力があるとされ、神さ
まに祈願する前に海水を浴びることがありました。⑦そのため、
海水からつくる塩にも同じ力があると考えられたのです。⑧相
撲の土俵に力士が塩をまきますし、そのほか神棚、かまどなど、
さまざまなものを清めるために、塩が使われてきました。

⑨現在でも、塩で清める習慣が残っています。⑩葬式から戻っ
たとき、家に入る前に塩をまく風習があります。⑪これは、死
のけがれを清めるためです。⑫また、料理屋の店先に塩を盛っ
てあることがあります。⑬すでに清めてあることと、いつでも
お清めできるように備えていることを表しています。

53. The First Food of the Season

①One popular event among many Japanese people in the old days was enjoying the first food of each season for the first time that year. ②These foods were called *hatsu-mono*, and it was said that a person's life bacome seventy-five days longer every time they ate *hatsu-mono*. ③In *Edo*, skipjack tuna caught for the first time that year were specially called *hatsu-gatsuo* and they appear in a famous haiku poem about early summer: "Green leaves in our sight / Cuckoo birds in the mountains / First skipjack tuna."

④There is also a traditional event for the first food of the season held by the Imperial family. ⑤*Niiname-sai*, in November, is an important Imperial ceremony at which the emperor offers the new rice of the year to the shrine inside the palace and then eats some while thanking the gods. ⑥New food is pure and has fresh power. ⑦It was thought that offering new food to the gods and eating it after that

130

brought good luck.
縁起がいい

⑧In some areas in Japan, people eat the first food of the

season while facing east. ⑨The first food changes with
　　　　東をむきながら　　　　　　　　　　　　　　　　　　〜とともに移り変わる

each season. ⑩At the beginning of a season, most people

eat the first food facing the direction of the sunrise for

better luck.
よりよい運気を求めて

---

53. 初物

①昔の人にとって、季節の食べ物をその年初めて味わうことは大きな楽しみの一つでした。②これを「初物(はつもの)」といい、「初物を食べると寿命が七十五日延びる」などといわれていました。③特に江戸で水揚げされる初物のカツオは「初鰹(はつがつお)」として珍重され、「目には青葉　山ほととぎす　初がつお」という、有名な初夏の俳句にもなっています。

④初物に関わる行事は、皇室の伝統にもみられます。⑤11月に行なわれる新嘗祭(にいなめさい)は、天皇がその年の新米(しんまい)を宮中(きゅうちゅう)の神殿に捧(ささ)げ、自らも食して神に感謝する、皇室の大事な祭儀です。⑥新しいものにはけがれがなく、新鮮な力があります。⑦それを神さまにお供(そな)えして、おさがりをいただくことは縁起がいいと考えられていたのです。

⑧「初物は東をむいて食べる」という地方もあります。⑨初物は、季節の移ろいを象徴するものです。⑩新しい季節の初めに、太陽がのぼる方向をむいて初物を食べることで、いっそういい運気を呼び込もうというものです。

54. Chopsticks

①*Hashi*, or chopsticks, had been holy tools for a religious
神聖な道具　　　　祭祀

service in which the Japanese people offered food to a god.
~を―に捧げた

②It was thought that chopsticks were tools to be used when

a god and human beings took a meal together.
人　　　　　　　食事をした

③*Hashi*, used at home in Japan, come to a point. ④Therefore
先が細くなっている

they can be used in many different ways such as holding
~をつまむこと

small things, cutting, and splitting. ⑤However, people have
~を裂くこと

to master how to hold them in the right way to be able to use
~を身につける　正しい箸の持ち方

them well. ⑥There is a special rule of etiquette which is
箸を上手に使う

different for each action from picking the chopsticks up to

putting them down.

⑦There are some things people must not do with *hashi*.
~でしてはならないこと

⑧Some examples are *koji-bashi*, when people take only

their favorite food from a dish that has many kinds of food

on it, and *sashi-bashi*, when people stab food such as
~を突き刺す

potatoes.

⑨*Wari-bashi*, half-split chopsticks, are used at restaurants
半分に割る箸(→割り箸)
and at homes when guests come. ⑩Since the old days, it is

common for the Japanese to have their own *hashi* which
ふつうの
they don't like others to use. ⑪It is thought that this is the

reason *wari-bashi*, the throwaway *hashi*, came to be used
使い捨ての
in Japan. (see pp.134-135)

---

54. 箸

①箸は古来、神さまに食べ物を捧げる儀式の祭器として使われ
た神聖なものでした。②箸は、神さまと人が一緒に食事をする
ための道具だと考えられていたのです。

③日本人が家庭で使っている箸は元が太く、先が細くなってい
ます。④そのため、小さいものをつまんだり、切ったり、裂い
たりと、さまざまな使い方ができます。⑤ただし、これを上手
に使いこなすには、正しい持ち方を身につける必要があります。
⑥持ち上げ方から置き方まで、細かな作法があるのはそうした
理由からです。

⑦箸でしてはいけないこともあります。⑧たとえば、料理が盛
られた皿から好物だけを選ぶ「こじ箸」、芋などを刺して食べ
る「刺し箸」などです。

⑨割り箸は、家庭に来客があったときや、料理屋などで使われ
ます。⑩日本では昔から自分の箸をもち、他人に使われること
を嫌いました。⑪割り箸は、この感覚から生まれたと考えられ
ています。

箸でしてはいけないこと

Things You Must Not Do with Chopsticks

こじ箸
Koji-bashi

皿に盛った料理をかき回して、自分の
好きなものを探す

Taking only your favorite food
from a dish that has many kinds
of food on it.

指し箸
Sashi-bashi

箸で料理をつき刺して、食べる

Stabbing food with chop-
sticks.

迷い箸
Mayoi-bashi

どの料理から手をつけようかと迷い、
料理の上で箸を動かす

Moving your chopsticks from dish
to dish while deciding what to eat.

踊り箸
Odori-bashi

箸をふりまわして話したり、人や物を指す

Talking while waving your chopsticks in the air or pointing them
at someone or something.

持ち箸
Mochi-bashi

二本の箸を握ったままの手で、器を持つ

Lifting up a dish with the hand
you are holding chopsticks with.

ねぶり箸
Neburi-bashi

箸先をなめたり、箸についたものをな
めてとろうとする

Sucking the pointed ends of the
chopsticks or removing the food
stuck to chopsticks with your
mouth.

洗い箸
Arai-bashi

食器の中の吸い物などで、箸の先を洗う

Washing the pointed ends of the chopsticks in soup, etc.

寄せ箸
Yose-bashi

箸を使い、食器などを手前に引き寄せる

Moving dishes closer using your chopsticks.

渡し箸
Watashi-bashi

食事中に箸を食器に渡して置く。これは「もういらない」という合図になり、失礼にあたる

Placing your chopsticks down across a dish during a meal. This means "I don't want any more," so it is rude.

立て箸
Tate-bashi

ご飯の中央に、箸を突き刺す。故人の枕元にそなえる形になるので縁起が悪い

Standing your chopsticks upright in your rice bowl. This brings bad luck because a similar thing is done at funerals.

拾い箸
Hiroi-bashi

箸から箸に食べ物を直接渡す。火葬場でお骨を拾うときのやり方を連想させるので嫌われる

Passing food from chopsticks to chopsticks. Japanese people avoid this because it is similar to when they pick bones out of the ashes of the dead at a funeral.

55. Straw-matted Flooring

①*Tatami*, or straw-matted flooring, is wonderful flooring unique
わらのマット床(→畳)　　　　　　　　　　　床材　　　～に独特の
to Japan, and this straw-matted flooring is suitable for Japan's
　　　　　　　　　　　　　　　　　　　　　　～に合っている
steamy climate. ②It is known that the Japanese people have been
湿度の高い気候
using *tatami* since ancient times because a small part of the
　　　　　　　　　　古代
oldest *tatami* in Japan is still kept at the *Shoso-in* treasure house
　　　　　　　　　　　　　　　　　　　　　～に保存されている正倉院
in *Nara* today. ③*Tatami*, at that time was not thick, but was more
　　　　　　　　　　　　　　　　　　　　　分厚い　　　より～のような
like today's *goza*, or thin straw mat. ④People folded them when
　　　　　　　　　　薄い　　　　　　　　　　　～を畳んだ
they weren't being used so they began to call them *tatami*, which
means something which is folded.
　　　　畳むもの
⑤In noble houses, in the *Heian* period, slightly thicker
　　貴族の家　　　　　　　　　　　　　　　少し分厚い
tatami were put down in some areas of the room where
　　　　～に敷かれた
people sat on or slept on. ⑥*Tatami* were put down wall-to-
　　　　　　　　　　　　　　　　　壁から壁まで敷きつめられた
wall for the first time in *Shoin-zukuri* style houses in the
　　　　　　　　　　　　　書院造りの家
Muromachi period. ⑦However, only rich families were able
to have wall-to-wall *tatami*. ⑧People in poor farm villages
　　　　　　　　　　　　　　　　　　　貧しい農村
usually used *mushiro*, made from straw and cattails, or
　　　　　　　　　　　　　　　　　　　　　　　　蒲

goza, made from stems of rushes instead of *tatami* flooring.
<u>イグサの茎</u>　<u>〜の替わりに</u>

⑨There is <u>a phrase</u>, "You need half a mat when you are
表現

standing and one mat when you are sleeping." ⑩The size of

tatami mats <u>depends on</u> the period and the area of Japan; but
<u>〜による</u>

in general, they are almost as long as a Japanese person's

average height.
平均的な背の高さ

---

55. 畳

①畳は湿度が高い気候に合った、日本独特のすばらしい床材です。②奈良の正倉院に、現存する日本最古の畳の残片が収められており、古代から畳が使われていたことがわかります。③その頃の畳は、厚みがなく現在のござのようなものでした。④普段はこれを畳んでおいたことから、畳という言葉が生まれたといわれています。

⑤平安時代の貴族の家では、座るところや寝るところに、やや厚みがある畳を部分的に敷いていました。⑥部屋中に敷きつめるようになるのは、室町時代に書院造りの建築物ができてからです。⑦しかし、それは裕福な家に限られていました。⑧貧しい農村では、わらや蒲で編んだむしろや、イグサの茎で織ったござが畳の替わりに使われていました。

⑨「立って半畳、寝て一畳」という表現があります。⑩畳1枚の大きさは、時代や地域により変化しますが、おおむね日本人の背丈にあった大きさになっています。

56. Small Alcove in the Living Room

①A *toko-no-ma*, or a raised alcove, about the size of one
　一段高くなった小部屋(→床の間)
tatami mat, is found at the back of a Japanese-style living
　　　　　　　　～の奥に見られる
room that has *tatami* flooring. ②The floor of the *toko-no-*
　　　　　畳敷きの～
ma is raised up about ten centimeters. ③Japanese people
　　　上げられている
place hanging scrolls on the back wall of the alcove and put
～をかける 掛け軸
a flower arrangement of the season at its center. ④Works of
　季節の生け花　　　　　　　　　　　　　　　　工芸品
art, such as an incense burner, are displayed on high and
　　　　香炉　　　　　　　　　　～に展示される
low shelves, called *chigai-dana*, on the right side of the
高低の棚(→違い棚)
alcove ⑤There is a paper door on the left side with a kind
　　　　　　　障子　　　　　　　　　　　　　　　　一種の
of small, narrow desk under it. ⑥This bay-window-like part
　　　　狭い　　　　　　　　　　　出窓のような
is called the *sho-in*, or study.
　　　　　　　書斎
⑦The *sho-in* is a built-in desk and was originally a place for
　　　　　　　　　つくり付けの～
monks to read books. ⑧Neither the *toko-no-ma* nor the *chigai-*
禅僧が本を読むための　　　～も―もない
dana serve their original purposes today. ⑨Now they are just
　　　本来の機能を果たす
a part of an architectural style as a space for accessories.
　　　　　　建築様式　　　　　　　　装飾品のための
⑩The architectural style that uses the *toko-no-ma*, *sho-in*,

and *chigai-dana* as a place for decorations is called the
飾りのための〜

sho-in-zukuri style. ⑪Living rooms with them are called
書院造り

ide-i or *zashiki*. ⑫Originally, *samurai* houses were built in

the *sho-in-zukuri* style. ⑬However, in the *Edo* period, this

style spread to the merchant and rich farmer class, too,
　〜に広まった

as a sign of family status. (see p.146)
その家の格式を示すものとして

---

56. 床の間

①床の間とは、日本建築の畳敷きの客間の正面にある、畳1枚分ほどの広さの空間です。②床の間は約10センチほど床が高くなっています。③正面の壁には掛け軸をかけ、中央には季節の生花を活けることになっています。④右手には違い棚と呼ばれる棚があり、香炉などの工芸品が置かれます。⑤左手には障子が立てられ、その下は幅が狭い机のようになっています。⑥この出窓のような部分が**書院**です。

⑦書院とはもともと、禅僧が書を読むためにつくられたスペースで、つくり付けの机でした。⑧床の間、違い棚も本来の機能は忘れられています。⑨それらは、装飾品を置くスペースとなり、建築様式の一部となりました。

⑩このように、鑑賞の場としての空間である床の間、書院、違い棚がある建築様式を「書院造り」といいます。⑪これらがある客間を「**出居**」とか「**ザシキ**」などと呼びました。⑫書院造りはもともと武家の様式でした。⑬しかし、江戸時代になると商家や裕福な農民の家にも取り入れられ、家の格式を示すものとして広まりました。

57. The Bath and Public Baths

①Foreigners say that the Japanese like taking baths.
外国の人々
②For the Japanese people, bathing is not only for cleaning
~だけでなく―もまた
the body but also for refreshing the mind and soul.
~を清めること
③In the old days, there were no bathtubs in Japan and the
湯船
Japanese word *furo* meant steam bath. ④An ancient steam
蒸気の風呂(→蒸し風呂)
bath was in a cave or other closed place where people
洞窟　　　　　閉ざされた場所
burned dry grasses, covered it with wet *mushiro* to fill it up
~を―で満たす
with steam, and washed off the dirt with it. ⑤A bathtub
汚れ
with hot water was later called *yuya* because it was

different from a steam bath.

⑥It is known that big bathtubs were built inside the *Horyu-*
大きな浴槽 (→浴堂)
ji and *Todai-ji* temples in the *Nara* period because people

thought cleaning the body with water would be rewarded
神によって報いられる(→功徳がある)
by the gods.

⑦Public steam baths first appeared in the *Edo* period.
登場した
⑧After that, public baths using bathtubs came to be built.
銭湯

⑨People often <u>made friends with</u> other people at public
　　　　　　　　〜と友だちになった
baths and they soon became <u>places to relax</u> in cities that
　　　　　　　　　　　　　　　憩いの場
people could not <u>do without.</u> (see p.147)
　　　　　　　　なしですます

57. 風呂と銭湯

①日本人はとても風呂好きだといわれています。②日本人の入浴には、体の汚れを落とすだけでなく、心を清めるという意味もあります。

③もともと日本には湯船につかる風呂はなく、「**風呂**」という言葉は**蒸し風呂**を指していました。④古代の蒸し風呂は、洞窟などで草木を燃やし、その上に濡らしたむしろを敷いて水蒸気を充満させ、体の汚れを浮かせるというものでした。⑤湯をためて入る風呂は「**湯屋**」といわれ、蒸し風呂とは区別されました。⑥仏教では、湯水で体を清めると功徳があるとされることから、奈良時代に法隆寺や東大寺で、浴堂がつくらたことが知られています。

⑦江戸時代になると、蒸し風呂の**銭湯**が登場しました。⑧その後、湯船がある銭湯がつくられるようになりました。⑨銭湯では人と人の交流が生まれ、都市に暮らす人々の憩いの場として、なくてはならないものになりました。

58. The Bathroom

①In the old days, the bathroom was called *kawa-ya*, or
便所
river place, because the Japanese people placed boards
川の場所   川に板を渡した
across rivers to answer the call of nature. ② However, it
自然が呼ぶ声に応える(→用を足す)
was common for the general public to answer the call of
庶民
nature on roadsides or at the edge of the village.
道端で   村はずれで
③Containers came to be used for toilets in the Middle Ages
便槽   トイレとして 中世では
in order to keep human waste as manure for the fields.
人間の排泄物   肥料   田畑
④*Zen* monks in the old days called this style of toilet

secchin, which still remains a term sometimes used for
用語   便所を指して使われることがある
bathrooms today.

⑤It is clear that there were wooden-box toilets in rooms
木の箱の便器
with *tatami* flooring in the *samurai* houses of the
畳敷きの部屋
Muromachi period.

⑥The Japanese thought that the toilet was unclean and
不浄な
called it *go-fu-jo*, or unclean place. ⑦As a result, it was

common for the bathroom to be built away from the main
～から離れて立てられた   母屋

house. ⑧On the other hand, the bathroom was also thought

to be the special space the god was in, and there is a custom
神が宿る特殊な空間
of visiting the bathroom with a newborn baby, called
新生児と便所を参る習慣
secchin-mairi. (see p.146)

---

58. 便所

①古くは川に板を渡し、そこで排泄したことから「厠（川屋）」などと呼ばれていました。②庶民は、道端や村はずれで用を足すのが一般的だったようです。

③中世になると糞尿が肥料に使われるようになったことから、排泄物を便壺に溜めておく、**くみ取り式の便所**が使われるようになりました。④便所を「雪隠」と呼ぶことがありますが、これはもともと禅僧がくみ取り式の便所を呼んだ言葉だとされています。

⑤室町時代の武家屋敷には、畳敷きの部屋に木の便器を設置したくみ取り式の便所があったことが知られています。

⑥「御不浄」と呼ぶことからもわかるように、便所は長いあいだ不浄な場所とされていました。⑦そのため、母屋とは別につくられるのが一般的でした。⑧その一方で、神が宿る特殊な空間とも考えられ、新生児といっしょに便所にお参りする「雪隠参り」などの習慣が生まれました。

59. Water

①In the old days, the Japanese people believed that water had spiritual power and water has continued to be used in many
靈力　使われ続けてきた
ceremonies and customs.
儀式　習慣

②For example, the Japanese people had a custom of drawing
~から水を汲むこと
water from a well and offering it to *Toshigami-sama*, the Year
井戸　~を―に供える
god, on the morning of January 1, called *waka-mizu*, or young water. ③People believed that they could become younger and keep off evil spirits by eating *zoni* made with this water.
~を祓う　邪気

④It was also a custom to take a bath in a washtub and wash
たらい　~をさらう
out wells on *tanabata* of the lunar calendar, which is in
旧暦の
early July on the solar calendar. ⑤This is because people
新暦の
wanted to wash away all the uncleanness left by the *tsuyu*,
不浄なもの　~にたまった
or rainy season, by the time the *Bon* Festival came.
~するときまでに　お盆がやってくる

⑥At the end of the *Bon* Festival, a ceremony of floating
霊を水に流す儀式(→精霊流し)
spirits on water takes place. ⑦People believed that water led
行なわれる　~へつながっていた
to the world of the spirits and they sent out the spirits of their
霊界　送り出す

ancestors to that world by floating *Bon* decorations on a river.
先祖　　　　　　　　　　　　　　　盆飾り

⑧Some people stand under a waterfall, called *taki-gyo*, to
　　　　　　　　　　　　　滝

get spiritual power from the god that is in the water.
　　　　　　　　　　　　水の中に棲む神

⑨Other than that, there are many religious ceremonies
　そのほか　　　　　　　　　　　　　宗教儀式

related to the spiritual power of water such as *misogi* in
〜に関係した

Shinto, in which people pour water over themselves to wash
　　　　　　　　　　〜を身体に浴びる　　　　　　　　〜を洗い流す

away their uncleanness.

---

59. 水

①日本では、古来、**水**には霊的な力があると信じられ、多くの儀式や習慣に取り入れられてきました。

②たとえば、1月1日の朝に、井戸から水を汲んで年神さまに供える「**若水**」という習慣がありました。③その水でつくった雑煮を食べると、若返りや邪気を祓うといった効用があると信じられていたのです。

④新暦の7月上旬にあたる旧暦の七夕には、家族で行水したり、井戸をさらったりする習慣がありました。⑤これは、梅雨のあいだにたまった不浄なものをお盆の前に清めるためのものです。

⑥お盆の最後には、**精霊流**しがあります。⑦水辺のかなたに霊界があると信じられ、盆飾りを川に流して、先祖を送り出したのです。

⑧滝の水に打たれる滝行は、水の神が棲む滝の水を浴びて霊力を得るための修行です。⑨そのほか、水を浴びて身を清める神道の「**禊**」など、水の霊力に頼る宗教儀式も多くみられます。

床の間
とこ ま

Small Alcove in the Living Room

床の間とは、畳敷きの客間の正面に、床を一段高く設けた空間で、通常、生け花や掛け軸など飾ります。その隣には、違い棚を設けます。

Small alcove is a raised-up space at the back of a *tatami*-floored living room. A flower arrangement and hanging scrolls are usually placed in it. There are high and low shelves next to it.

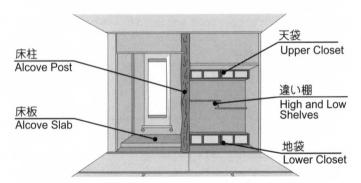

床柱
Alcove Post

床板
Alcove Slab

天袋
Upper Closet

違い棚
High and Low Shelves

地袋
Lower Closet

武家屋敷の便所

The Bathroom of Samurai Houses

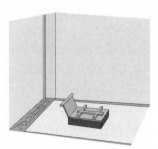

畳敷きの小部屋の中央に木製の便器があり、その下に汚物をためておく、汲み取り式の便所。

There were wooden-box toilets, which were used as containers to keep waste, at the center of *tatami* rooms.

風呂と銭湯

The Bath and Public Bathes

江戸時代の五右衛門風呂
Goemon Bathtub of the Edo period

竈の上に鉄釜を据え置いてスノコを敷き、まわりは木桶で囲んだものです。

A big iron pot on an old Japanese-style stove surrounded by wood with a drainboard on the bottom.

江戸時代の銭湯
Public Baths of the Edo period

女湯の様子。湯船は石榴口といわれる奥の入り口の中にあります。

This is a picture of a female bath. The bathtub is inside an entrance called *zakuro-guchi* located at the back of the building.

60. Midsummer and Year-end Gifts

①It is a tradition for the Japanese to give *chugen*, a
midsummer gift, and *seibo*, a year-end gift, to people they
真夏の贈り物　　　　　　　　　年末の贈り物
have close relationships with.
とても親しい関係にある
②In China, *chugen* along with *jogen* and *kagen*, was one of
　　　　　　　　　　　　～と並んで
the three days people celebrated the birthdays of the three
　　　　　　　　　～を祝う
great gods of Taoism, *Shi-fuku*, *Sha-zai* and *Kai-yaku*. ③On
　　　　　　　道教
July 15th of the lunisolar calendar, people made a fire and
　　　　　　　　旧暦の
prayed to be forgiven for their sins. ④In the *Edo* period in
　　　　　贖罪されること
Japan, this Chinese custom changed into the custom of giving
presents to others around the time of the *Bon* Festival and
　　　　　　　　　～の頃に　　　　　　お盆
soon became popular.
やがて
⑤The word, *seibo*, originally only meant "year-end". ⑥It
was a custom to offer something to the spirit of their
　　　　　　　　　　　　　　　　　　先祖の霊
ancestors in the new year. ⑦Later, the word, *seibo*, had a
meaning for people to give gifts to their parents and others
at the end of the year. ⑧In the *Edo* period, the s*amurai*
　　　　　　　　　　　　　　　　　　武家階級

class began to give gifts to the people they had close

relationships with. ⑨This custom later became popular

among government officials in the *Meiji* period.
　　　　　役人
⑩These Japanese traditions of giving food or beverage as
　　　　　　　　　　　　　　　　　　　飲食物
gifts comes with the idea that they give vitality to the
　　～という考え方を伴う　　　　　生命力を注ぐ
people who receive them.
それらを受け取る人たち

---

60. 中元と歳暮

①夏の**中元**と暮れの**歳暮**は、どちらも普段からお世話になっ
ている人へ贈り物をする習わしです。

②中国では、「中元」は「上元」、「下元」と並び、道教の三人
の大帝（賜福大帝、赦罪大帝、解厄大帝）の誕生を祝う「三元節」
の一つでした。③旧暦7月15日には火をたき、贖罪を祈るし
きたりでした。④これが江戸時代に日本で広まり、お盆の頃に
贈り物をする習慣に変わりました。

⑤「歳暮」は、もともとは年末を意味しました。⑥新年に先祖
の霊に供物を届ける習慣がありました。⑦のちに、歳暮は歳
末に親などに贈り物をすることを意味するようになりました。
⑧江戸時代になると、年末に武士が世話になった相手などに贈
答をするようになりました。⑨これが、明治時代に役人の間に
広まりました。

⑩このような日本の贈り物のしきたりは、飲食物の贈り物は相
手の生命力を高めるという考え方からきたものです。

61. Ceremonial Folded Paper and Colored Paper Strings

①The Japanese use *shugi-bukuro*, ceremonial envelopes,
儀式的な封筒(→祝儀袋)
for giving gifts of money such as for a wedding. ②*Noshi, a*

ceremonial folded paper, is attached to the upper-right part
儀式用に折られた紙　　　　　～に付けられる　　　右上部分に
of the *shugi-bukuro* and *mizu-hiki*, or colored paper strings,
色のついた紙のひも(→水引)
are tied together at the center. ③*Noshi* means *noshi-awabi*,
真ん中に
which is thought to bring good luck. ④*Noshi-awabi* is
幸運
abalone that has been sliced thin, stretched, and dried in
鮑　　　　　　　薄く切られた　のばされた　　　　　乾燥させた
order to be offered to the gods. ⑤The *noshi* on the *shugi-*

bukuro is modeled after *noshi-awabi*, which is wrapped in
～を模している
hexagonal paper.
六角形の
⑥The *mizu-hiki* at the center of the *noshi-bukuro* is a bundle
～の束
of strings made by twisting, pasting, and drying thinly cut
～をよること ～にのりをつけること　　　細く切った紙片
pieces of paper. ⑦Gold, silver, red, and white strings are

used for the *shugi-bukuro*. ⑧There are also black strings

that are used for *bu-shugi-bukuro*, or sympathy envelopes.
悔やみの封筒(→不祝儀袋)
⑨*Shugi-bukuro* and *bu-shugi-bukuro* differ not only in color
～においてだけでなく

but also in the number of strings　and in the knot. ⑩In the
_{―においてもまた　ひもの数　　　　　　　結び目}

case of *shugi-bukuro*, an odd number of strings are tied in a
_{奇数の　　　　　　　　　　蝶結びにする}

bow because odd numbers are thought to be good luck. ⑪On

the other hand, in the case of *bu-shugi-bukuro*, an even
_{偶数の}

number of strings are tied tightly.　(see p.156)
_{固く結ばれた(→結び切りされた)}

(see p.156)

---

61. のしと水引

①結婚などのお祝い金は**祝儀袋**（しゅうぎぶくろ）に入れて渡します。②この祝儀袋の右上には「**のし**」が付き、真ん中に「**水引**」（みずひき）が結ばれています。

③のしは、縁起物とされている熨斗鮑（のしあわび）を表します。④熨斗鮑とは、鮑を薄く切ってのばして乾燥させたもので、神さまにお供（そな）えするものです。⑤祝儀袋に付いているのしは、六角の紙に包まれた熨斗鮑を象徴化したものです。

⑥袋の中央に結ばれている水引は、細く切った紙をよったものに水のりをひき、乾かしてつくった複数のひもの集合体です。⑦祝儀袋に使われるのは、金、銀、赤、白です。⑧黒いものもあり、これは**不祝儀袋**に使われます。

⑨祝儀と不祝儀では、色だけでなく使う水引の本数や結び方も違います。⑩祝儀袋には、縁起がいいとされている奇数の水引を**蝶結び**にします。⑪一方、不祝儀袋には、偶数の水引を**結び切り**にします。

62. A Square Piece of Cloth to Wrap and Carry Things

①A *Furo-shiki* , just a square piece of cloth, is very useful
正方形の布

because it can be used to wrap and carry various shaped
～を包んで運ぶ　　　さまざまな形のもの

things such as boxes and long bottles.

②Because a piece of cloth called *hira-tsutsumi*, the origin
原型

of *furo-shiki*, is kept at the *Shoso-in* treasure house, we
正倉院

know that people used cloth to wrap something like clothes
衣類のような物

as far back as the *Nara* period.
～までさかのぼって

③Some people say the word, *furo-shiki*, came to be used in
使われるようになった

the *Muromachi* period. ④According to this idea, a feudal
大名

lord, who was invited to a bath built by *Ashikaga*
～に招かれた

Yoshimitsu, wrapped his clothes in a piece of cloth before
自分の衣類

the bath and then stood on the cloth while he put his clothes
～しているあいだ　～を着た

on after the bath. ⑤This cloth came to be called *furo-shiki*,

or bath mat.
風呂の敷き物

⑥These days, people rarely wrap their things in a *furo-*
最近は　　　　　　　ほとんど～しない

shiki. ⑤However, it is polite to bring wedding presents,
～するのが礼儀正しい　　婚礼の祝い品

funeral offerings, and so on, wrapped in a *furo-shiki*.
弔事の香典
(see p.157)

62. 風呂敷

①**風呂敷**は、ただの正方形の布ですが、箱のようなものからビンのように縦長のものまで、形を選ばずに包んで運べる、大変に便利なものです。

②正倉院の宝物の中にも、衣類を包んだとされる「**平つつみ**」と呼ばれる布があり、奈良時代から布でものを包む習慣があったことがわかります。

③風呂敷という言葉の語源は、室町時代にあったという説があります。④足利義満が建てた湯屋に招かれた大名が、入浴するときに脱いだ衣類を布で包んでおき、風呂からあがるとこれを敷いて着替えたということです。⑤そのことから、風呂敷と呼ばれるようになったとするものです。

⑥最近は、荷物を風呂敷で包むことは少なくなりました。⑦しかし、今でも婚礼の祝い品や弔事の香典は風呂敷で包んで持参するのが礼儀です。

63. New Year's Postcards

①In the old days, the Japanese had a custom of visiting

their neighbors' houses to greet them for the New Year.
近所の家　　　　　　　～に挨拶する

②The families who had visitors treated them to *iwai-zake*,
訪問客があった　～に―をもてなす

celebratory *sake*, and *osechi-ryori*, food for New Year's.
祝い酒

③In this way, people got together to enjoy talking and
集まった

having a meal for celebration. ④ The custom of visiting
祝いの膳

neighbors' houses is dying out now because people began
なくなりつつある

working for companies in big cities and don't have to be
会社勤め　　　　　　大都市で　　　　　　それほど～ない

friendly with their neighbors as much.
～と親しくする

⑤Sending New Year's postcards is a new custom started

after the mailing system was created in the *Meiji* period.
郵便制度

⑥This custom has taken root in Japan because it is cheap
根づいてしまった

and easy to exchange New Year's greetings by mail.
～を交わす

⑦People sometimes send formal New Year's postcards to
儀礼的な

people they are not so close with and tell them how they are
それほど親しくない

doing. ⑧Since many people stopped visiting each other at
～なので　　　　　　訪問するのをやめた

New Year's, they become <u>more distant in their relationships.</u>
　　　　　　　　　　疎遠になる　　　　　　人間関係
⑨Today, many people don't even send New Year's cards but

send New Year's emails.

---

63. 年賀状

①日本のお正月には、新年を迎えると家々をまわり、新年の挨拶をする習慣がありました。②訪問を受けた方は、祝い酒をふるまい、正月のおせち料理でもてなしました。③こうして人々が家に集まり、にぎやかに祝いの膳を囲んだものでした。④しかし、会社勤めの人が増えるにつれて地域のつながりが薄れ、年始回りの習わしはなくなりつつあります。

⑤**年賀状**は明治時代に郵便制度が確立したことによって生まれた、比較的新しいしきたりです。⑥安く、しかも簡単に**年始の挨拶**ができるので、すっかり人々のあいだに浸透しました。

⑦あまりつき合いのない人に、儀礼的に年賀状を出し、年に一度の近況報告をすることもあります。⑧逆に年賀状を出すことで挨拶に行かなくなり、人間関係が希薄になっている面もあります。⑨最近は、はがきではなく電子メールで年賀状を送る人も増えています。

のし袋と水引き

Ceremonial Folded Paper and Colored Paper Strings

お祝いのときに金銭を入れて贈る袋。のしと水引きがついています。

Ceremonial envelopes for giving gifts of money for happy events. These envelopes have ceremonial folded paper and colored paper strings.

慶事には、裏の重なる部分を上向きにします（①）。弔事には逆に、重なる部分を下向きにします（②）。

Place the upper end of the paper under the lower end for happy events(Fig 1).
On the other hand, place the lower end of the paper under the upper end for sad events (Fig 2).

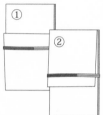

蝶結び
Cho-musubi

何度繰り返してもよい、婚礼以外のお祝い事に使います。

This is used for happy events which take place many times except for weddings.

あわび結び
Awabi-musubi

結び切りの一種。末永いおつき合いをしたい気持ちを込めて婚礼などで使います。黒白の水引きは葬儀にも使います。

This is used for wedding to hope for a long lasting relationship. We can use this for unlucky events with black and white strings.

結び切り
Musubi-kiri

強く結びほどけないので、繰り返さないほうがいい婚礼祝いや快気祝いに使います。

Very tight knot used for event which nobody wants to repeat such as wedding and recovery from sickness.

風呂敷の包み方
How to Wrap Things in a Furo-shiki

慶事（右包み）
Happy Events

左側をたたみ上下右の順にたたむ
Fold the left corner followed by upper, lower, and right.

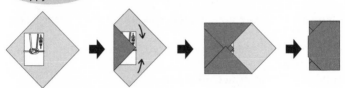

弔事（左包み）
Unhappy Events

右側をたたみ上下左の順にたたむ
Fold the right corner followed by upper, lower, and left.

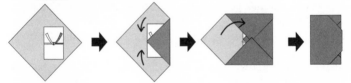

箱の包み方（隠し包み）
How to Wrap a Box

①品物を置き、柄を合わせて位置を決める

Place the box according to the pattern of the fu-ro-shiki.

②柄の部分をもとに戻し、手前の部分で品物をくるむ

Unfold the upper corner and bring the lower corner over the box.

③左右を整えて真結びする

Pull across the right and left corners to meet together and tie.

④柄の部分の布を整える

Straighten the upper corner.

⑤真結びの上にかぶせる

Bring the upper corner over the knot.

157

64. Shrines

①In Japan, each area, such as villages and towns, has its
[たとえば～]
own shrine. ②The god of each area is called *Ujigami-sama*,
[神社]
the protecting god, and people who believe in this god are
[守る神 (→氏神)]   [～を信仰する]
called *uji-ko*, or protected children.
[守られる子ども(→氏子)]
③The Japanese people have many traditions for every season and for

important times in a person's life. ④Most of them have something to
[人生の重要な時点]   [～と関係がある]
do with the *Ujigami-sama* god. ⑤Speaking of traditions for every

season, they begin with *hatsu-mode*, followed by the *haru-matsuri*,
[～で始まる]
where people pray for good crops, and the *aki-matsuri*, where people
[豊作を祈願する]
thank the gods for good crops. ⑥In addition, traditions for important
[それに加えて]
times in a person's life include *miya-mairi*, which is held for 30-day-
[～を含む]
old babies, *shichi-go-san*, which is the celebrations for 7,5,3 years

old, and so on. ⑦Apart from these traditions, people with bad luck
[～とは別に]   [運の悪い人]
sometimes visit a shrine to get purified.
[お祓いをしてもらう]
⑧There are some traditional rules when people visit a
[伝統的な作法]
shrine. ⑨People must wash their hands before they pray.
[お祈り]

⑩They stand before the altar, bow once, and ring a bell.
拝殿　　　　　　　　一礼する

⑪Next, they throw an offer of money, usually coins, into a
賽銭

box and take two deep bows. ⑫Then, they join their hands
深い礼　　　　　　　両手を合わせる

together and clap twice. ⑬Finally, they pray to the god and
拍手をする　　　　～に願い事をする

bow deeply once more. ⑭This is called *ni-hai-ni-hakushu-*

ichi-hai, two bows, two claps and one bow. (see p.166)
二拝二拍手一拝

---

64. 神社

①日本には、村、町など、それぞれの地域に必ず**神社**がありま
す。②地域の神さまは**氏神さま**と呼ばれ、それを信仰する住民
は「氏子」と呼ばれています。

③日本には、季節や人生の節目に応じてさまざまなしきたりが
あります。④その多くは氏神さまに関わったものでした。⑤季
節のしきたりは新年の初詣に始まり、豊作を祈願する春祭り、
収穫に感謝する秋祭りと続きます。⑥一方、人生の節目の行事
としては、出生から約 30 日後の**お宮参り**、三歳、五歳、七歳
の**七五三**などがあります。⑦そのほか、悪いことが続くと神社
にお参りし、お祓いをしてもらうこともあります。

⑧神社に参拝するときは、決められた作法があります。⑨お祈
りする前には、必ず手を洗います。⑩それから拝殿の正面に立
ち、一礼してから鈴を鳴らします。⑪**賽銭箱**に賽銭を投げ入れ、
2 度深く頭を下げます。⑫次に両手を合わせてから 2 回パンパ
ンと音をたてて拍手をします。⑬願い事をしたあと 1 回深く礼
をします。⑭これを「**二拝二拍手一拝**」といいます。

65. The Shinto Altar

①In the old days, there was a *Shinto* altar in almost every
神棚
farm house and merchant house in Japan. ②A *Shinto* altar
農家　　　　　　商家
is usually placed on a shelf on the wall near the ceiling.
棚　　　　　壁　　　　　天井
③On this shelf, people put a *tama-gushi*, a branch of a holy
神聖な木の枝(→玉串)
tree, that the *Ujigami-sama* god gave them and a *taima*, a

talisman of the *Ise-jingu* shrine. ④Placed in the center of
伊勢神社のお札　　　　　神棚の中央に小さな社があり[→倒置]
the shelf is a small shrine, modeled after the shrine, in
　　　　　　　　　　　　　～を模した(小さな社)
which people put a *taima* and the *Ujigami*'s talisman. ⑤A

branch of *sakaki* and a *go-shinto*, a candle for gods are
神さまのためのロウソク(→御神灯)
placed on both sides and a holy rope is stretched across the
しめ縄　　　　　張られている
front.

⑥People offer *sake*, rice, water, salt and so on to their *Shinto* altar

every morning. ⑦These offerings are called *shinsen*, or food for

the gods. ⑧Fish and vegetables may be offered on special days

like New Year's and on the 1st and 15th of each month
正月
⑨The rules for praying at a *Shinto* altar are the same as for
　　　　　　　　　　　　　　　　　　　　　～と同じ

160

regular shrines, *ni-hai-ni-hakushu-ichi-hai*, two bows, two

二拝二拍手一拝

claps and one bow. ⑩In the old days, pious families used to

信心深い

pray to their *Shinto* altar many times a day.

⑪Today, few families have a *Shinto* altar because people

are losing their belief in this custom and because many

失いつつある　　　　　信仰

people live in Western-style houses. (see p.166)

洋風の家

---

65. 神棚

---

①古い日本の農家や商家には、必ずといっていいほど**神棚**があ
りました。②神棚というのは天井近くに作られた棚です。③そ
こは氏神さまからいただいた**玉串**や伊勢神宮の大麻などを置
く場所です。④中央には神社を模した小さな社があり、この中
に大麻や氏神さまのお札を納めます。⑤左右には榊と御神灯
があり、前方にはしめ縄がかけられています。

⑥神棚には毎朝、酒や米、水、塩などを供えます。⑦これらは、
神饌と呼ばれ、神さまの食べ物とされています。⑧また、正月
や毎月1日・15日といった特別な日には、魚や野菜なども供
えることがあります。

⑨神棚にお参りする作法は、神社をお参りするときと同じ「二
拝二拍手一拝」とされています。⑩昔は、信心深い家庭では、
毎日、何回も神棚をお参りする習慣がありました。

⑪最近は人々の信仰心が薄れると同時に住宅が洋風になったた
め、神棚がある家が少なくなりました。

66. Visiting a Grave

①Many Japanese visit the graves of their ancestors during
墓　　　　　　　　　　　先祖
higan, the equinoctial weeks in spring and fall, and for
昼夜の等しい週(→彼岸)
o-bon, the *Bon* Festival. ②They also visit graves on the
お盆
anniversary of their ancestor's deaths. ③Visits on
先祖の命日　　　　　　　　　　　　　　訪問
anniversaries are for holding a mass just for that certain
ミサ(→礼拝、供養)
ancestor or relative and visits during *higan* and *o-bon* are

for holding a mass for all the family ancestors or relatives,

not just for a certain person.
特定の人のためではなく
④Some Japanese graves only have the family name on
名字
them. ⑤The word "family" here includes distant ancestors,
含む　　　　遠い先祖
as well as close relatives, like a grandfather. ⑥Graves
〜だけでなく　近い親戚
which have words such as "peace", "love" or "wind"
和　　　　　愛　　　　　風
instead of family names are often seen these days, too.
〜の代わりに
⑦When people visit their family grave, they clean them.

⑧They weed, rake up fallen leaves and clean the
雑草を抜く　落ち葉を掃く　　　　　　　　　　　墓石
gravestone. ⑨Then, they offer incense sticks or other
〜を供える　線香

objects to their ancestors and pray for them. ⑩The offering
食べ物の供物

of food at graves is also a common custom of the Japanese.
日本の習慣

(see p.167)

66. 墓参り

①春と秋の彼岸やお盆には、多くの人が**墓参り**に行きます。②また、故人の**命日**にも墓参りに行きます。③命日の墓参りは故人の供養ですが、お盆や彼岸の墓参りは特定の故人だけでなく、ご先祖さまを供養するという意味合いが強いものです。

④日本の墓石には、「○○家先祖代々之墓」と書かれたものがあります。⑤この「先祖」には、たとえば自分の祖父といった身近な人だけでなく、何代か前に死んだ先祖も含まれます。⑥最近は家名の代わりに「和」、「愛」、「風」などと刻まれた墓石も多くなっています。

⑦墓参りでは、まず墓の掃除から始めます。⑧雑草を抜き、落ち葉を掃いて、墓石をきれいに磨きます。⑨そして、供物を供え、線香をあげて祈ります。⑩供物として食べ物を供えるのが、一般的な日本の習慣です。

67. The Buddhist Altar

①A *Shinto* altar is the place to put an *o-fuda*, or *Ujigami*'s
神棚
talisman and a *taima*, or a talisman of the *Ise-jingu* shrine.
お札   伊勢神宮のお札
②On the other hand, a Buddhist altar has a small platform
仏壇   小さな段
to put Buddha statues and spirit tablets on. ③In old, large
~を置く 仏像   位牌
houses there was a room called the *butsu-ma* where a big

Buddhist altar was placed. ④Today, many Japanese people

live in smaller apartments so they buy a small Buddhist

altar to put on a chest of drawers or wherever they have
箪笥   場所があればどこでも
space.

⑤It is said that Buddhist altars spread widely due to the
広まった   ~によって
ji-dan-seido system in the *Edo* period. ⑥This system forced
寺檀制度   ~に―をさせた
all people to belong to temples. ⑦As a result, an *i-hai*, or
~に属する   その結果
spirit tablet, was made by temples when someone died and

people needed a Buddhist altar to put the spirit tablet in.

⑧A grave is a place to put the bones of ancestors but a
墓   遺骨   先祖
Buddhist altar is the place for the spirit tablet to rest. ⑨It
納める

is tradition for people to offer incense sticks to the Buddhist
線香
altar and pray for the people they knew. (see p.167)
〜を供養する

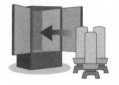

67. 仏壇

①神棚はお札や大麻を置くための棚です。②それに対して、仏壇は本尊や先祖の位牌を納めるための段です。③昔の大きな家には、仏間と呼ばれる部屋が設けられ、そこに大きな仏壇が置かれていました。④現在は、多くの人が場所に余裕がないアパートやマンションで暮らすため、箪笥の上に置いたり、どこでも置くことができるような小型の仏壇が多くなっています。⑤仏壇の普及は、江戸時代の寺檀制度がきっかけだったといわれています。⑥この制度により、誰もが寺の檀家になることを義務づけられました。⑦身内が死ぬと位牌がつくられるので、それをしまっておく仏壇が必要になったのです。

⑧墓が先祖の遺体を納める場であるのに対して、仏壇は位牌を祀る場です。⑨そこで、生前面識があった人が死んだ家を訪れるようなとき、仏壇に線香をあげ、故人を供養する習慣があります。

神社参拝の作法

How to Visit a Shrine

①鳥居の手前で一礼する
Bow once in front of the shrine gate.

②参道は中央を避けて歩く
Avoid walking down the center of the path to the shrine.

③手水舎で手を洗い口をすすぐ
Wash your hands and gargle with holy water.

④賽銭を入れる
Put in an offering of money.

⑤鈴をならす
Ring the bell.

⑥おじぎを深く二度する
Take two deep bows.

⑦手を胸の高さで二回打つ
Clap your hands twice in front of your chest.

⑧深くおじぎをする
Bow deeply.

神棚

The Shinto Altar

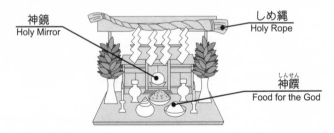

神鏡
Holy Mirror

しめ縄
Holy Rope

神饌
Food for the God

古い家で見かける神棚は、氏神さまからいただいた玉串や、伊勢神宮の大麻を置く場所です。

The *Shinto* altar, which is often seen in old houses, is the place to display the branch of a holy tree received from the protecting god and a talisman of the *Ise-jingu* shrine.

墓参りの作法

How to Visit a Grave

①準備するもの
Things to prepare.

②墓石とそのまわりを清める
Clean the gravestone and the area around it.

③花立に花を入れる
Put flowers in the flower vases.

⑥手を合わせて拝礼する
Join your hands together and pray.

⑤墓石の上から水をかける
Pour water on the gravestone.

④供物をそなえ線香をあげる
Offer something and burn incense sticks.

仏壇

The Buddhist Altar

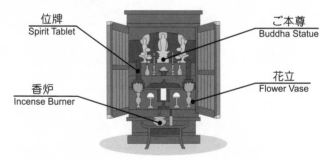

位牌
Spirit Tablet

ご本尊
Buddha Statue

香炉
Incense Burner

花立
Flower Vase

仏壇には、先祖の位牌やご本尊を納めます。

A Buddhist altar is the place for spirit tablets of ancestors and Buddha statues to rest.

鶴の折り方

How to Make a Paper Crane

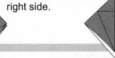

①三角に折る

Fold the paper into a triangle.

②半分に折る

Fold the triangle in half again.

⑤内側を広げて正方形になるように折る

Open the triangle to make a square again.

④ひっくり返して反対側に折る

Turn it over and bring the left tip of the base to the right side.

③内側を広げて正方形になるように折る

Open the triangle to make a square.

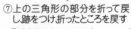

⑥真ん中の線にあわせて折る

Fold it in half at the center.

⑦上の三角形の部分を折って戻し跡をつけ折ったところを戻す

Fold the top part down and then bring it back up.

⑨ひっくり返して先ほどと同様に折る

Turn it over and do the same to the other side.

⑧内側を広げて菱形ができるように折る

Open the square to fit it to this shape.

⑩中心にむけて折る
Fold it in half at the center.

⑪ひっくり返す
Turn it over.

⑫同様に中心にむけて折る
Fold it in half at the center again.

⑬脇を広げて中に割り上に折る
One folded leg at the bottom becomes the head and the other becomes the tail. Open one of the legs and fold it in half so it points upward.

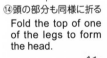

⑭頭の部分も同様に折る
Fold the top of one of the legs to form the head.

⑮もう一方も脇を広げて同じに折る
Do the same to the other leg.

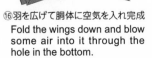

⑯羽を広げて胴体に空気を入れ完成
Fold the wings down and blow some air into it through the hole in the bottom.

The Art of Folding Paper / 折り紙

Origami is a traditional Japanese art in which people fold various figures out of one square piece of paper. The purpose of *origami* is not only for fun but also for ceremonial uses such as *noshi*, a ceremonial folded paper.

Origami paper can be folded into many different shapes. Cranes, *samurai* helmets, boats and balloons are well known. People sometimes present *sen-ba-zuru*, a thousand folded paper cranes, to someone who is sick because the crane is a symbol of long life and people believe that folding a thousand paper cranes will help that person get well.

　折り紙は、1枚の正方形の紙からさまざまな形をつくる日本の伝統的な工作の一つです。「折り紙」には遊びを目的としたもののほかに、熨斗などのような儀礼のためのものがあります。

「折り紙」の折り方は数多くありますが、鶴、兜、舟、風船などがよく知られています。なかでも長寿のシンボルである鶴の折り紙は、「千羽鶴」といって千羽折ることで病気がよくなると信じられ、病人へのお見舞いとして贈られることがあります。

Chapter 4

Traditions for Fortune and Taboos

··

第4章
縁起と禁忌のしきたり

68. Good Luck Arrows

①Many Japanese people make their first visit of the year to
　初詣
shrines on New Year's Day to pray for a new year of peace
　　　　元日　　　　　　　　　～を祈る　平和で幸せな新年
and happiness and to get a *hama-ya,* or good luck arrow,
　　　　　　　　　　　　　　　　　　　幸運の矢(→破魔矢)
with the hope their prayers will come true. ②They keep
～という望みを込めて　　願い事
this arrow in their house for one year and return it to the
shrine the following New Year's Day.
　　　　翌年の元日
③People believed that arrows had magical and spiritual
　　　　　　　　　　　　　　　　　　呪術的な　　　　霊的な
powers to keep away evil because they could kill enemies
　　　　　悪魔を祓う　　　　　　　　　　　　　倒す　敵
and game that were out of their reach. ④Therefore arrows
獲物　手の届かない範囲の
have always been used in various ceremonies.
　　　　　　　　　　　　さまざまな
⑤*Jarai,* an event at which people walk around and shoot
　　　　　　　　　　　　　　　　　歩き回った　　　　的を射た
arrows at targets, was introduced as a New Year's ceremony
in *the Chronicles of Japan.* ⑥At the Imperial palace, the
　　『日本書紀』
meigen-no-gi ceremony, in which people flicked a bow
　　　　　　　　　　　　　　　　　　　弓をはじいた
without an arrow to make a sound, was held when princes
were born, and so on. ⑦As time went by, such ceremonies
　　　　　　　　　　　時が過ぎるにつれて

spread among the general public.
~のあいだに広まった　庶民

⑧It is thought that *hama-ya* arrows came from the arrows used in the *Jarai* ceremony. ⑨These arrows eventually came to be sold at shrines as good luck charms.(see p.180)
ついには
縁起物

68. 破魔矢

①多くの人が、初詣に出かけると、新しい1年の無事を願い、また願いを込めて縁起物の**破魔矢**をいただきます。②これを1年間家に置き、翌年の初詣のときに神社に納めます。

③矢は、遠くにいる敵や獲物を手を触れずに倒すことができることから、呪術的な力、悪魔を祓う霊力があると考えられました。④そのため、多くの儀式に使われてきました。

⑤『日本書紀』には、徒歩で的を射る「射礼」が正月の儀式として紹介されています。⑥また、宮中では、矢を使わずに弓をはじいて鳴らす「鳴弦の儀」という儀式があり、皇太子が誕生したときなどに行なわれてきました。⑦こうした儀式は、時の流れとともに民衆のあいだにも広まっていきました。

⑧破魔矢は、射礼の儀式に使われた矢からきたものと考えられています。⑨それが、縁起物として神社で売られるようになりました。

69. The Dharma Doll

①In Japan, the winner of an election painting in the eye of
　　　　　　　　　　　　　　　選挙　　　　　目を描き入れている
a dharma doll is a common sight on TV. ②There are no
達磨人形　　　　　　　よく見る光景
eyes on a new dharma doll at first. ③People paint one eye

first and wish for something and then paint the other eye

when that wish comes true.
　　　　希望がかなう
④It is said that dharma dolls came from the Chinese *shukoshi*,

which was something like a human-shaped wooden spinning
　　　　　　　　　　　　　　　　人の形をした　　　　　　　　独楽
top that was played with at drinking parties. ⑤*Shukoshi* later
　　　　　　　　　　　　　　　酒の席で
came to be made from paper in the Ming period in China.
　　　　　　　　　　　　　　　　　明の時代
⑥It was called *futo-o*, an undying man, after it came to Japan
　　　　　　　　　　倒れない男(→不倒翁)
and many thought it was a good luck charm for youth and
　　多くの人　　　　　　　　　縁起物　　　　　　　　　不老長寿
long life. ⑦It always stands up quickly after it is pushed over
　　　　　　　　　　　　　　　　　　　　　　　　　　倒される
because it is made from paper and its bottom part is heavy.
　　　　　　　　　　　　　　　　　　底の部分
⑧The name *futo-o* was changed to dharma in the *Edo*

period. ⑨The name dharma comes from the Buddhist saint
　　　　　　　　　　　　　　　　　　　　　　　達磨大師
Dharma, the founder of the *Zen-shu* sect. ⑩The name was
　　　　　禅宗の開祖

changed to "dharma" because of an ancient Chinese event
<u>～により</u>　　　　<u>中国の故事</u>

where saint Dharma sat in *Zen* meditation in a cave for nine
　　　　　　　　　　<u>座禅を組んでいた</u>　　　　<u>洞窟</u>

years and <u>became enlightened</u> and then, many people
　　　　　<u>悟りを開いた</u>

thought he was <u>worthy of</u> the name, *futo-o*. ⑪Many people
　　　　　<u>～に値した</u>

think of it as a good luck charm because it always stands

up quickly after being pushed over.(see p.180)

---

69. 達磨

①日本では、選挙で当選した候補者が**達磨**（だるま）に目を入れている映像が、テレビニュースで流れることがあります。②買ったばかりの達磨には目が描（えが）かれていません。③願い事を込めてまず片目を描き、それが成就（じょうじゅ）したときにもう一方の目を描きます。

④達磨の原型は、中国の**酒胡子**（しゅこし）という、人の形をした木製の独楽（こま）のようなもので、酒の席での遊びに使われていたといわれています。⑤その酒胡子は、明の時代になると、紙で作られるようになりました。

⑥これが日本に伝わると、**不倒翁**（ふとうおう）と呼ばれ、不老長寿を祝う縁起物とされました。⑦紙で作られ、底を重くしてあるため、倒してもすぐに起き上がるからです。

⑧不倒翁が達磨となったのは、江戸時代のことです。⑨達磨とは禅宗の開祖である**達磨大師**です。⑩達磨大師が９年間洞窟で座禅を組み続けて悟りを開いたという故事が不倒翁と重なって、現在のような達磨となりました。⑪倒してもすぐに起き上がることから、しだいに縁起物とされるようになりました。

70. Welcoming Cat

①A *maneki-neko*, or welcoming cat, is a cat-shaped doll
  歓迎する猫(→招き猫)
sitting with one paw raised, and it is a good luck charm for
  片手を上げている   縁起物
business success.
商売繁盛
②There are different ideas about where the *maneki-neko*
                                    招き猫がどこから来たか
came from but the most famous idea is the *Gotoku-ji* temple
                                              豪徳寺
story. ③*Gotoku-ji* temple is still in *Setagaya*, *Tokyo* today.

④In the *Edo* period, when *Ii Naotaka*, the second head of
                                        彦根藩第二代藩主
the *Hikone* domain, was passing by the *Gotoku-ji* temple on
                      ～を通りかかっていた
his way home from hawking, a cat beckoned him. ⑤He
                    鷹狩り   ～に手招きした
followed the cat into the temple to rest when it started to
                              休憩するために すると～
rain and lightning hit the gate of the temple. ⑥*Naotaka* and
          ～に雷が落ちた
his servants believed they narrowly escaped the lightning
    家来   危うく～を逃れる   雷
thanks to the temple. ⑦They were so happy that the *Ii*
～のおかげで   井伊家
family decided to join the *Gotoku-ji* temple.
            ～の檀那になる
⑧The *Gotoku-ji* temple was poor at that time but it soon

became rich thanks to the *Ii* family's help. ⑨The cat was
栄えた

dedicated to the temple as the symbol of good luck and
〜に祀られた　　　　　　　　　　　　幸運のシンボルとして（→招福観音）

became the *maneki-neko*.

⑩Some people say that the origin of the *maneki-neko*
　　　　　　　　　　　　　　〜の起源

began at the *Jisho-in* temple and others say that it began in
　　　　　　　自性院

the red-light district of *Yoshiwara*. ⑪However, there is no
赤線区域(→遊郭)

proof either of these stories is true.(see p.181)
証拠　　　どの〜も―ない

---

70. 招き猫

①**招き猫**とは、片手を上げた猫の人形で、商売繁盛の縁起物と
されています。

②招き猫の由来にはいくつかの説がありますが、なかでも有名
なのは豪徳寺説です。③豪徳寺というのは東京世田谷区に現
存する寺です。④江戸時代、彦根藩第二代藩主の井伊直孝が
鷹狩りに出かけた帰りに豪徳寺の前を通りかかると、1匹の猫
が手招きしました。⑤誘われて寺に入り休憩していると、にわ
かに大雨が降り始め、やがて山門に落雷しました。⑥直孝一行
は、この寺のおかげで難を逃れることができたと思いました。
⑦そのため、彼らは喜び、井伊家はこの寺の檀那になりました。
⑧当時の豪徳寺は、貧しい寺でしたが、井伊家の支援によって
栄えるようになりました。⑨手招きした猫は招福観音として
祀られ、これが招き猫になったという説です。
⑩そのほかにも、新宿にある自性院という寺や、吉原の遊郭
に起源があるとするなど、さまざまな説があります。⑪しかし、
どれも確証はありません。

71. The Seven Lucky Gods

①*Shichi-fuku-jin*, the Seven Lucky Gods, are made up of
七柱の幸運の神さま (→七福神)　　　　　～からなる

Daikoku-ten, *Hotei-son*, *Fukuroku-ju*, *Bishamon-ten*,

Benzai-ten, *Juro-jin* and *Ebisu*. ②Since the old days, they

have been believed in as gods that bring good luck.
信仰されてきた　　　　　　　　　　　　～をもたらす

③It is thought that *Ebisu* was the first of the seven that the

Japanese started believing in. ④Then, in the *Kamakura*

period, people came to believe in *Daikoku-ten*, the god of

good crops, and *Benzai-ten*, the goddess of art and wisdom,
豊作　　　　　　　　　　　　　　女神　　　　　　芸能　　知恵

too. ⑤In additon, people in the *Muromachi* period started
それに加えて

believing in *Bishamon-ten*, the god of morals, *Hotei-son*,
道徳

the human form of the Buddhist saint *Miroku*, *Fukuroku-ju*,
～の化身　　　　　菩薩

the symbol of long life, and *Juro-jin*, the god of long life.
長寿

⑥These seven gods came to be named *Shichi-fuku-jin*.
～と名づけられるようになった

⑦Among them, the only original Japanese god is *Ebisu*.
日本固有の

⑧*Daikoku-ten*, *Bishamon-ten* and *Benzai-ten* are gods of

ancient India and *Hotei-son*, *Juro-jin* and *Fukuroku-ju* are
古代インド

gods of ancient China. ⑨A typical characteristic of
古代中国　　　　　　　　　典型的な特徴

traditional Japanese faith is the belief in not only gods of
伝統的な日本人の信仰　　　　　　　　　〜だけでなく―もまた

Japan but also gods of India and China, as well. ⑩In many
　　　　　　　　　　　　　　　　　　　〜も同様に

pictures of *Shichi-fuku-jin*, they are on a treasure ship.
　　　　　　　　　　　　　　　　　　　宝船

⑪This is probably because Japan is an island country.
　　　　　　　　　　　　　　　　　　島国

(see p.181)

---

71. 七福神

①「七福神」とは、大黒天、布袋尊、福禄寿、毘沙門天、弁財天、寿老人、恵比須の七柱の神さまを指します。②七福神は、福を招く神々として信仰の対象とされてきました。

③これはもともと、恵比須信仰に始まったものだと考えられています。④鎌倉時代になると、五穀豊穣の神である大黒天と芸能や知恵を司る弁財天がこれに加わりました。⑤室町時代になると、人倫の道を司る毘沙門天、弥勒菩薩の化身とされる布袋尊、幸福、長寿を象徴する福禄寿、長寿の神である寿老人が加わりました。⑥このようにして、「七福神」となりました。⑦この中で日本古来の神は恵比須だけです。⑧大黒天、毘沙門天、弁財天は古代インドの神、布袋尊、寿老人、福禄寿は中国の神です。⑨日本の神だけでなく、インドや中国の神も一緒になっているところは、日本の民俗信仰の特徴を表わしています。⑩七福神の絵では、七柱の神が宝船に乗っています。⑪これは日本が海に囲まれた島国だからなのでしょう。

破魔矢

Good Luck Arrows

魔を祓う霊力があるとされていた矢は、魔よけとして正月の縁起物になっています。

Arrows, which people believed to have spiritual powers to keep away evil, are used as a good luck charm for New Year's today.

絵馬

The Votive Picture of a Horse

神の乗り物である馬の代わりに、馬の絵を奉納したことに始まる縁起物です。

This picture of a horse became a good luck charm to replace the offering of a real horse, which people thought to be transportation for the gods.

達磨

The Dharma Doll

願掛けの縁起物。願いを込めて左目を描き、それがかなったとき右目を描きます。

A good luck charm used to wish for something. People paint left eye first and wish for something and then paint right eye when that wish comes true.

招き猫

Welcoming Cat

商売の縁起物とされる、片手を上げた猫の人形です。左手を上げた猫は人を招き、右手を上げた猫はお金を招くといわれています。

It is believed to be a cat-shaped good luck charm for business success. A cat with its left paw raised welcomes people and one with its right paw raised welcomes money.

七福神

The Seven Lucky Gods

福禄寿
Fukuroku-ju

頭が長い長寿の神

The long-headed god of long life

恵比須
Ebisu

商売繁盛の神

The god of business success

寿老人
Juro-jin

鹿を連れた中国の神

The Chinese god with a deer

大黒天
Daikoku-ten

豊作をつかさどるインドの神

The Indian god of good crops

布袋尊
Hotei-son

大きな腹をした福の神

The potbellied god of wealth

毘沙門天
Bishamon-ten

戦をつかさどるインドの神

The Indian god of war

弁財天
Benzai-ten

音楽や学問の女神

The goddess of music and studies

72. The God of Bathrooms

①In the old days, the Japanese thought there was a god at bathrooms. ②Many traditions about childbirth or newborn babies have something to do with the bathroom because many people believed that the god of bathrooms protected childbirth.

③In many areas of Japan, for example, legend has it that the mother will have an easy birth or will give birth to a cute baby if she cleans the bathroom. ④In some areas, there is a custom called *secchin-mairi*, where people take their newborn baby to the bathroom. ⑤For this custom, people take their baby, at three or seven-days old, to the bathroom and pray.

⑥People in some areas believe in the custom of having a thank-you ceremony for their bathroom between New Year's Eve and New Year's Day. ⑦For this ceremony, people clean their bathroom, offer it a meal and then all the family members say thank you to the bathroom.

⑧In this way, the bathroom is not only a place to <u>answer</u>

<u>the call of nature</u> for the <u>Japanese</u> but a place which <u>is</u>
自然の呼び声に応える(→用を足す)　日本人

<u>thought of as religiouly</u> special.
〜と考えられた　信仰的に

---

72. 便所の神

①古くから便所^{べんじょ}には神さまがいると考えられていました。②**便所の神さまは、お産を守る神である**と広く昔から信じられていたため、お産や新生児に関するしきたりには便所にまつわるものが多くあります。

③たとえば、妊婦が便所をきれいに掃除するときれいな子が生まれるとか、安産になるという伝承が各地にみられます。④地方によっては、生まれて間もない子どもを便所に連れて行く、「雪隠参り^{せっちんまい}」などと呼ばれる便所参りの習慣があります。⑤生後3日あるいは7日の子どもを便所に連れて行き、お参りさせる習慣です。

⑥大晦日から正月にかけて、便所にお礼の儀式をする地方もあります。⑦きれいに掃除してお膳を供え、家族そろって便所に感謝の言葉をのべるものです。

⑧このように便所は単に排泄^{はいせつ}の場というだけでなく、信仰的に特別な場所として大切に扱われてきたのです。

73. Eating a Sushi Roll Facing the Lucky Direction of the Year

①Nowadays the custom of eating a large *sushi* roll facing
太巻き
the lucky direction, or *e-ho*, of the year on *setsubun*, the
幸運な方角 (→恵方)
day when winter turns to spring, is popular. ②*E-ho* means
冬が春に変わる日
the direction which the *Toshigami-sama* god is in that year and
年神さまのいる方向
is decided by the Chinese zodiac sign of the year. ③Facing the
えと
lucky direction and eating an entire large *sushi* roll while
全部の
silently making a wish is called *e-ho-maki*.
願いをしながら
④It is thought that the old custom of *e-ho-mairi*, visiting

shrines located in the lucky direction of the year at New
恵方にある神社を訪れること
Year's, came back in the form of this custom done at
〜の形で復活した
setsubun.

⑤There are various ideas about the origin of *e-ho-maki*.
さまざまな意見   起源
⑥One of them is that merchants in *Osaka* began *e-ho-maki*
商人
to pray for business success in the late *Edo* period or in the
〜を祈って 商売繁盛
early *Meiji* period. ⑦This custom was not practiced for a
行なわれなかった   しばらく
while after that but was started again in the late *Showa*

period. ⑧It is said it began again through a campaign run
~によって行なわれたキャンペーン
by a seaweed merchant cooperative association in *Osaka* in
海苔問屋協同組合
the 52nd year of *Showa*. ⑨This custom of *e-ho-maki* came
昭和52年に
back to life and took root all over Japan again because of a
生き返った　　　　　根づいた
promotional campaign for seaweed and the sales strategy of
海苔の販売促進キャンペーン　　　　　　　　　　販売戦略
a convenience store chain.(see p.192)
あるコンビニチェーン

---

73. 恵方巻き

①最近、節分の日にその年の「恵方（えほう）」をむいて、太巻きを食べる風習が注目されています。②「恵方」というのはその年の年神さまがいる方向で、えとによって決まります。③その方向をむき、願い事を思い浮かべながら無言で太巻きを丸かじりするのが、「恵方巻き」です。

④これは、正月に行なわれていた「恵方参り」が形を変え、節分のしきたりとして復活したものと考えられます。

⑤恵方巻きの起源にはさまざまな説があります。⑥そのうちの一つが江戸時代の末期から明治時代初期に、大阪の商人が商売繁盛の祈願のために始めたという説です。⑦一時期は忘れられていましたが、昭和の末期から再び行なわれるようになりました。⑧そのきっかけとなったのは、昭和52年、大阪の海苔問屋（のりどん）協同組合が行なったキャンペーンだといわれています。⑨昔の習俗を掘り起こした、海苔の販売促進キャンペーンと、コンビニチェーンの宣伝戦略により、恵方巻きの習慣は再び全国的に定着することになりました。

74.Construction Site Purification Ceremony

①*Jichin-sai* is a *Shinto* ceremony, usually held on a lucky
神道の儀式　　　　　　　　　　　大安
day, at a construction site before building starts. ②The
建設用地　　　　　　　　　　　　施主
owner of the site, along with the building designer and
　　　　　　　　　～とともに　　設計者
constructing workers, asks a *Shinto* priest to pray to the
工事関係者　　　　　～するよう頼む 神主　　　　～に一を祈る
god of land for the safe construction and protection of the
土地の神さま　　　　　　　工事　　　　～を守ること
building.

③Before the ceremony, four green bamboo branches with
　　　　　　　　　　　　　　葉のついた青竹
leaves are set up in a square surrounding the center of the
　　～が立てられる 四角く　　～を囲んで
site. ④Holy ropes are stretched between the four corners of
　　しめ縄　　　　～の間に張られる　　　～の四つの角に
the bamboo branches. ⑤Inside the square of holy ropes is
　　　　　　　　　　　　　　～の内側
believed to be a holy area. ⑥An altar is prepared at the
　　　　　　　神聖な場所　　　祭壇
center of this square and a *himorogi* made from a branch of
sakaki with hemp and *shide*, or many long and thin pieces
　　　　　　麻　　　　　　　たくさんの長く細い紙(→紙垂)
of paper is set up. ⑦This is the place the god will come
down to.

⑧First, the *Shinto* priest purifies all the people there.
　　　　　　　　　　　　　　～を清める

186

⑨Then, the god is invited down to the *himorogi* and the
〜に招かれる
people offer *shinsen*, or food for the gods, while praying for
〜を供える　　　　　　　　　　　　　　　〜を祈りながら
the safe construction and protection of the building.

⑩Next, the designer, the owner and the chief of construc-
　　　　　　　　　　　　　　　　　　　　　　工事の責任者
tion spade the ground a little. ⑪Finally, they pray again and
土地に鍬を入れる
then see the god off. (see p.192)

---

74. 地鎮祭

①地鎮祭（じちんさい）とは、建物を建てるときに行なわれる神道（しんとう）の儀式で、通常は大安（たいあん）の日に行なわれます。②施主（せしゅ）が神主（かんぬし）に依頼して設計者、工事関係者とともに、土地の神さまに工事の安全と建物の守護を祈願するものです。

③準備として、建物をたてる土地の中央を囲むように葉のついた青竹を４本立てます。④青竹の四角の辺の部分にしめ縄を張っておきます。⑤しめ縄で囲まれた部分は、神聖な場所となります。⑥その中央には、祭壇をつくり、榊（さかき）に麻（あさ）と紙垂（しで）をつけた神籬（ひもろぎ）を立てます。⑦これが神さまが降りてくる場所です。

⑧まずは、神主さんがお祓いし、参加者全員を清めます。⑨次に、神さまを神籬にお招きし、神さまの食事となる神饌（しんせん）をお供（そな）えして、工事の安全と建物の守護を祈願します。⑩続いて、設計者、施主、工事の責任者が土地に鍬を入れます。⑪そして、再び祈りを捧（ささ）げた後、神さまをお送りして、終了します。

75. The Six-day Calendar System

①*Roku-yo*, introduced from China in the *Muromachi*
　　　　　　　　～から伝えられた
period, is a six-day calendar system which shows whether a
　　　　　　　6つの曜日のカレンダーシステム(→六曜)　　　　　　　　　～であるかどうか
day is lucky or not. ②There are 6 kinds of days called *sen-*

sho, *tomo-biki*, *sen-bu*, *butsu-metsu*, *tai-an* and *shakko*.

③According to the *roku-yo* system, January 1st of the lunar
　　～によると　　　　　　　　　　　　　　　　　　太陰暦(旧暦)
calendar is *sen-sho*, January 2nd is *tomo-biki*, January 3rd

is *butsu-metsu*, and so on.

④Each day of *roku-yo* has its own meaning. ⑤For example,
　　　　　　　　　　　　　　　　　　意味
butsu-metsu is believed to be an unlucky day. ⑥The Japanese

don't like to hold any happy events, like weddings, on that
　　　　　　　行なう　　　　　　　　　　　結婚式
day. ⑦Funerals are not held on *tomo-biki* because people

believe that the dead person will take his or her friends with
　　　　　　　　　　　　　　　　　～を連れて行く
them. ⑧Therefore most of the funeral halls and crematories,
　　　　　　　　　　　　　　葬祭場　　　　　　　火葬場
places that burn the body to ashes, are closed on *tomo-biki*.
死体を焼いて灰にする場所
⑨In the *roku-yo* system, the 6 kinds of days are simply

assigned to the calendar in order so, in reality, there are no
～に割りふられた　　　　　順番に　　　現実には

real reasons why *butsu-metsu* days are unlucky, and so on.

⑩Nevertheless, this *roku-yo* system became popular among
にもかかわらず

the superstitious general public from the late *Edo* period.
迷信深い　　　　　庶民

⑪Even today, there are quite a few calendars which have
少なくない

roku-yo days labeled in small letters along with the date of
小さな字でラベルを貼られた　　　〜とともに

the solar calendar. (see p.193)
太陽暦(新暦)

(see p.193)

---

75. 六曜

①**六曜**とは暦に付属してその日の吉凶を示すもので、室町時代の初期に中国から伝わったとされています。②「**先勝**」、「**友引**」、「**先負**」、「**仏滅**」、「**大安**」、「**赤口**」の六つがあります。③旧暦の１月１日を「先勝」とし、２日が「友引」、３日が「仏滅」と、割り振ったものです。

④六曜には、それぞれ意味があります。⑤たとえば、「仏滅」はよくない日とされます。⑥この日は結婚式などの祝い事を避けます。⑦また、「友引」は「友を引く」とされ、葬式はこの日を避けます。⑧そのため、多くの葬祭場や火葬場が休みになります。

⑨六曜は日付に機械的に割りふったものなので、「仏滅」が悪い日という根拠はありません。⑩にもかかわらず、縁起を担ぐのが好きな日本の庶民の間に江戸時代の末期から広まりました。⑪日付とともに小さな字で六曜が書かれているカレンダーは、現在でも少なくありません。

76. Unlucky Years and Driving off Evil

①The Japanese word *yaku* means unluckiness. ②The Japanese
不幸　　　　　　　　　　　　　　　　　　日本人
believe those who are a certain age in the *yaku-doshi*, or
～の人
unlucky year, will have the unluckiest year in their life. ③This
人生で最も不幸な年を過ごす
idea came from China and it is thought that it spread with the

theory of the positive and negative in the *Heian* period.
陰陽道
④In the old days, when a person turned 13, 25, 37, 49 or 61 in *kazoe-doshi*,
（～歳に)なった
calendar year, their zodiac sign and the animal sign of that year were the
数え年　　　　彼らのえと　　　　　　その年のえと
same, and people regarded these ages as yakudoshi, or unlucky years.
～とみなす
⑤However, people today think that the ages of 25 and 42 for men
～歳の
and the ages of 19 and 33 for women are unlucky years. ⑥These

unlucky years are called *hon-yaku*, or the main unlucky years.

⑦The year before *hon-yaku* is called *mae-yaku* and the year
前年　　　　　　　　　　　　　　　　　　　　　　　　　翌年
after is called *ato-yaku*. ⑧It is believed that people are likely to
～になりがちである
be unlucky during these three years. ⑨The year for men turning

42 and women turning 33 is called *tai-yaku*, the unluckiest year,

so those people must be most careful at that time in their life.
そのとき、一生で最も注意しなければならない

⑩People in *yaku-doshi* have the evil driven off themselves
　　　　　　　邪悪なものをお祓いをしてもらう

so that they won't be unlucky. ⑪It is common to get
〜にならないように

purified at shrines or temples. ⑫Other purifications in some
祈禱を受ける　　　　　　　　　　　　　厄払い

areas in Japan involve dropping personal belongings on the
　　　　　　　　〜を含む　〜を落とすこと　　　持ち物

street on New Year's Eve or *setsu-bun*, or having a party
　　　　大晦日

with a lot of people and handing out money. (see p.193)
　　　　　　　　　　　　　　お金をまく

(see p.193)

---

76. 厄年と厄払い

①「厄」とは災いという意味です。②そして、厄年は一生のうちで災いが多いとされる年齢のことです。③中国から伝来した考え方で、平安時代以降に陰陽道によって広まったと考えられています。

④もともとの厄年は、13歳、25歳、37歳、49歳、61歳であり、生まれた年と同じえとの年で数え年でかぞえていました。⑤これがいつしか変化して、現在は男性が25歳と42歳、女性が19歳と33歳とされています。⑥この年齢は「本厄」です。⑦そして、その前年を「前厄」、次の年を「後厄」と呼びます。⑧この3年間は災いが起こりやすいとされています。⑨また、男性の42歳と女性の33歳は「大厄」と呼ばれ、一生でもっとも注意しなければならない年齢とされています。

⑩厄年の災いを避けるために、「厄払い」をします。⑪神社や寺に行って祈禱してもらうのが一般的です。⑫そのほか、大晦日や節分に当人が身につけていたものを道の辻に落とす、人を集めて宴を催す、お金をまくといったことをする地方もあります。

恵方巻き

Eating a Sushi Roll Facing the Lucky Direction

節分の日に、その年の年神がいるとされる恵方
の方向をむいて、太巻きを食べる習慣です。

It is a custom to eat a large sushi roll on the
day when winter turns to spring while facing
the lucky direction, which the *Toshigami-sama*
god is in, that year.

地鎮祭

Construction Site Purification Celemony

建物をたてる前に、土地の神さま
に、工事の安全と建物の守護を祈
ります。

People pray to the god of land for
the safe construction and protection of the building before construction starts.

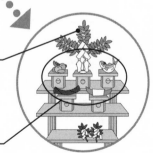

神籬
The Branch of Sakaki with
Hemp and Many Long and Thin
Pieces of Paper

神饌
Food for the God

厄年
やくどし

Unlucky Years

厄年とは、一生のうちで災いが
多いとされている年齢です。男
性と女性で異なります。

It is believed that people will
have the unluckiest year in
their life. The years that are
unlucky differ for men and
women.

男性 / Men		
前厄 Mae-Yaku	本厄 Hon-Yaku	後厄 Ato-Yaku
24歳 (Age)	25歳	26歳
41歳	42歳	43歳
60歳	61歳	62歳

女性 / Women		
前厄 Mae-Yaku	本厄 Hon-Yaku	後厄 Ato-Yaku
18歳 (Age)	19歳	20歳
32歳	33歳	34歳
36歳	37歳	38歳

六曜
ろくよう

The Six-day Calendar System

カレンダーに書かれている六曜は、その日の吉凶を示します。

The six different kinds of days of this calendar system show
whether that day is lucky or not.

急ぐのがよい日。午前は吉で午後は凶

The day you should act quickly. It has a lucky morning with
an unlucky afternoon.

先勝
せんしょう
Senshou

赤口
しゃっこう
Shakkou

正午のみ吉で午前中と午後は凶。火の元や刃物に注意

This day has a unlucky morning, lucky at noon, and unlucky
afternoon. You should be careful about fire and edged tools.

朝は吉正午は凶。夕方は大吉

This day has a lucky morning, unlucky at noon, and a
very lucky evening.

友引
ともびき
Tomobiki

大安
たいあん
Taian

何をやってもうまくいく大吉の日

Everything goes well.
This is the luckiest day.

平静を保ち勝負事や急用を避ける
日。午前は凶で午後は吉

The day you should calm down and
keep away from games of chance or
urgent business. It has an unlucky
morning with a lucky afternoon.

先負
せんぶ
Senpu

仏滅
ぶつめつ
Butsumetsu

何事もよくない大凶の日

Nothing goes well. This is
the unluckiest day.

77. One Hundred Prayers at a Shrine or Temple

①*Hyaku-do-mairi* is one of the ways the Japanese visit a
　　　　　　　　　　　 ～する方法の一つ

shrine or temple to wish for something big. ②People walk
　　　　　　　　　　　　　大きな願い事をするために

from a shrine's gate to its altar or from a temple's gate to its
　　　　 神社の門　　　　　　拝殿　　　　　　寺の門

main hall one hundred times while praying, each time, for
本堂　　　　　　　　　　　願い事がかなうように祈りながら

their wish to come true. ③It is believed that doing this

barefoot has more of an effect. ④While they do this, people
裸足で　　　より効果がある

do things like put a small stone down every ten times so
　　　　　　～のような　　　　　　　　　　　10回ごとに

that they won't forget the number of trips they have taken.
　　　　　～を忘れないように　　　　　　　　　終えた往復

⑤On the other hand, visiting a shrine or temple to pray
　　一方

every day for one hundred days is called *hyaku-nichi-mode*.

⑥*Hyaku-do-mairi* is a scaled-down version of *hyaku-nichi-*
　　　　　　　　　　　　　　　　 ～の短縮版

mode and is done when people have little time. ⑦When a
　　　　　　　　　 ～するときに行なわれる

mother prays for her daughter to give birth safely or when
　　　 ～が—するように祈る　　　　　　無事出産する

people pray for a family member who is at death's door to
　　　　　　　　　死の扉の前にいる(→重体の)家族

get well again, they often do *hyaku-do-mairi*.

⑧If the wish comes true, people offer money or other

things to the shrine or temple. ⑨This is called *o-rei-mairi*,

visiting a shrine or temple to give thanks, or *gan-hatashi*,
感謝するために神社や寺を訪れる(→お礼参り)
making a wish come true.
願い事をかなえること(→願はたし)

77. 百度参り

①「**百度参り**」とは、大きな願い事があるときに神社や寺にお参りする方法です。②神社の場合は門と拝殿、寺では門と本堂のあいだを1日に100往復して、1度ごとに願い事がかなうように祈ります。③履物を脱いで、裸足でこれを行なうと、効果が大きいとされています。④そして、回数を忘れないように、たとえば10度に一つずつ小石を置いておきます。

⑤願い事があるとき、100日間お参りを続けることを「**百日詣**」といいます。⑥百度参りは、時間が差し迫っているときにこれを短縮したものだと考えられています。⑦母親が自分の娘が無事に出産するように祈るときや、生死のあいだをさまよう家族の無事の回復を祈るようなとき、百度参りをすることがありました。

⑧百度参りで願いがかなうと、神社にお金やものを奉納することになっています。⑨これは「**お礼参り**」とか「**願はたし**」と呼ばれています。

78. Visiting a Shrine to Make a Curse at 2:00 a.m.

①*Ushi-no-koku-mairi* is an old Japanese ceremony in which people visit a shrine at *ushi-no-koku*, about two o'clock in the morning, to put a curse on someone.
〜に呪いをかける

②People pretend that a straw doll is the person they hate
〜とみなす　　藁人形　　　　　　　　恨んでいる人
and nail that doll to the shrine's holy tree with a long nail
〜を一に釘で打つ　　ご神木　　　　　　　　　長い釘
called *go-sun kugi*. ③It is believed the person they hate will die if this is done for seven nights in a row.
連続して

④People also believe they can hurt the part of the body
〜を傷つける
they nail. ⑤For example, the person they hate will get a headache if they nail the head of the straw doll to the tree.
頭が痛い

⑥However, it is believed that they must not be seen by any other people when doing *ushi-no-koku-mairi*. ⑦They will not be able to curse the person they hate and something bad
何か悪いこと
will happen to themselves if they are seen. ⑧That is why
そのため
people do it around two o'clock in the morning when most other people are asleep at home.
寝ている

⑨The *Kifune-jinja* shrine in *Kyoto* has been a well-known
　貴船神社　　　　　　　　　　　　　　　　　　〜でよく知られてきた場所

place for *ushi-no-koku-mairi* since the ancient times.

---

78. 丑の刻参り

①「丑の刻参り」とは日本に昔から伝わる呪いの儀式で、真夜中の丑の刻（午前2時ごろ）に行なうことから、こう呼ばれるようになりました。

②恨みを持つ相手に見立てた**藁人形**を神社のご神木に5寸釘で打ち込みます。③これを7日間続けると相手は死ぬといわれています。

④また、打ち込んだ部位に痛手を与えることができるともいわれています。⑤たとえば、藁人形の頭に打ち込むと頭が痛くなるなどというようにです。

⑥ただし、丑の刻参りは、他人に見られてはいけないとされています。⑦もしも他人に見られると、呪いが無効になるだけでなく、災いが自分に降りかかるのです。⑧深夜の丑の刻に行なうのは、そうした理由からです。

⑨京都にある貴船神社は、昔から丑の刻参りの舞台として知られています。

79. Tossing Offerings of Money at a Shrine

①The Japanese toss offerings of money, usually coins, into
日本人　　　　～を投げる　お金のお供え(→賽銭)
a donation box when they visit a shrine. ②Normally, it is
賽銭箱　　　　　　　　　　　　　　　　　ふつうは
very bad manners to toss money. ③If people toss money to

a sales clerk at a shop, the sales clerk will probably get
店員
angry. ④In spite of this, why do people toss offerings of
これにもかかわらず
money at shrines?

⑤Well, it is needless to say that money has economic value
それは　～は言うまでもない　　　　　　　経済的価値がある
but offerings of money also have a symbolic meaning. ⑥It
象徴的な意味
is believed that the sins, uncleanness and bad luck of people
罪　　けがれ　　　　災い
can be transferred to money. ⑦Tossing some money into a
～に託されることができる
clear pond or a fountain probably came about as an act to
きれいな池　　　泉　　　　　　　～する行為として起こった
purify or wash away that person's unclean money.
～を清める　～を洗い流す　　　　けがれたお金
⑧Shrines are thought of as places to purify people's sins
～を清める
and uncleanness. ⑨It is believed that, when people donate
～を寄付する
money at shrines, they are transferring their uncleanness
～を—に託している
and bad luck to the money they offer, toss it away and

purify themselves.

79. 神社で賽銭を投げる

①神社にお参りするときには、**賽銭**を投げることになっていま
す。②一般的に考えると、お金を投げつけるというのは、決し
て礼にかなった行為ではありません。③店で買い物をしたとき、
代金を投げつけたら、店員は怒ってしまうに違いありません。
④にもかかわらず、神さまに向かって賽銭を投げつけるのはな
ぜでしょうか。

⑤お金は、経済的な価値があることはいうまでもありませんが、
象徴的な意味も持っています。⑥お金は、人々が罪やけがれ、
災いを託すものでもあるのです。⑦よく、きれいな池や泉にコ
インが投げ込まれていることがありますが、これはけがれたお
金を清めたいという衝動からなのでしょう。

⑧一方、神社は罪やけがれを祓い清めてくれる浄化場所と考え
ることができます。⑨人々は、自分のけがれや災いを賽銭に託
して、神社や寺で投げ捨てて清めているのだと考えられます。

80. No Stepping on Thresholds

① These days, people like flat floors and there are many
　　最近は　　　　　　　　　　　　　　平らな床
barrier-free buildings. ② Raised thresholds are rarely seen
バリアフリーの　　　　　　　　　高い敷居　　　　　　ほとんど見られない
in new houses today. ③ However, they can still be seen in

older houses today.

④ In the old days, the Japanese believed they must not step
　　　　　　　　　　　　　　　　　　　　　　　　　　　　　　　　　　　　～を踏む
on thresholds and often said, "Stepping on a threshold is
—
like stepping on your parent's head."

⑤ Another thing people believed they must not step on was
　ほかのもの
the border of a *tatami* mat. ⑥ It was true that people must
畳のふち　　　　　　　　　　　　　　確かに～
not step on a *tatami* border because some *tatami* borders

had family emblems on them. ⑦ However, that was not the
　　家紋
only reason.
唯一の理由
⑧ Both thresholds and *tatami* borders are borders between
　　　　　　　　　　　　　　　　　　　　　　　　　　　　境界
one area and another. ⑨ It is thought these borders became
　　　　　　　　　　　　　　　　　　　　　　　　タブーになった
taboo because they were not part of a definite place and did
—　　　　　　　　　　　　　　　　　　　　　明確な　　　　　　　　　—
not belong to either area. ⑩ This also may be the same
どちらの領域にも属さない

reason <u>why</u> it was believed that <u>scary things</u> happened at
～である理由　　　　　　　　　　　　　　　怖いこと

the borders of villages and <u>why</u> there were also <u>a small</u>

<u>stone statue of *Jizo*</u>, a Buddhist saint, or <u>small shrines</u>
地蔵(菩薩)の小さな石像　　　　　　　　　　　　　　祠

dedicated to god placed there to protect the people.
～を祀った

80. 敷居を踏んではいけない

①最近はバリアフリーが取り入れられ、建物の床に凹凸をつけることを嫌います。②そのため新しい家には目立った「敷居」はほとんど見かけなくなりました。③しかし古い家には、一段高くなった敷居があります。

④昔は、この敷居は踏んではいけないものとされ、「**敷居を踏むのは親の頭を踏むのと同じだ**」などといわれていました。

⑤同じように踏んではいけないものに、畳のふちがあります。⑥畳のふちに家紋がついていることがあるので、踏まないようにするという意味もありました。⑦しかしながら、それだけではないようです。

⑧敷居も畳のふちも、ある空間とほかの空間の境界です。⑨境目は、あちらでもなくこちらでもない不安定な場所なので、こうしたタブーが生まれたのではないかと考えられます。⑩村はずれに怖い話があり、人々を守護する地蔵や、神を祀った祠があることがありますが、これも同じような理由からなのでしょう。

81. Do Not Cut Fingernails at Night

① These days, you rarely hear the saying, "Do not cut your
〔ほとんど~ない〕 〔ことわざ〕 〔「夜に爪を切ってはいけない」〕
fingernails at night," but people in the old days often said

this.

② Unlike today, night was lit by only the moonlight and was
〔今日と違って〕 〔~で照らされて〕〔月明かりだけで〕
very dark in the old days, so people usually went to bed at

sunset. ③ People used to be afraid of the dark and they
〔~を恐れる〕 〔暗闇〕
believed monsters and other evil spirits came around.
〔妖怪〕 〔悪霊〕 〔行き来した〕

④ So, why must people not cut their fingernails at night?
〔それでは〕

⑤ Well, cutting tools are used when people cut their
〔それはね〕 〔刃物〕
fingernails. ⑥ People believed cutting tools had spiritual
〔霊力〕
power and could be used to keep evil away.
〔魔よけのために〕

⑦ At the same time, people believed this spiritual power of
〔それと同時に〕
the cutting tools made a gap in their body when they used
〔隙〕
them. ⑧ People believed that the active monsters and evil
〔活発な〕
spirits could enter their body through any gaps made by the
〔~に入る〕
cutting tools if they were used at night.

81. 夜に爪を切ってはいけない

①最近はあまり耳にすることもなくなりましたが、昔はよく「**夜に爪を切ってはいけない**」といわれたものです。

②今と違い、昔の夜は月明かりだけの闇の世界であり、日が暮れると眠るのが普通でした。③人々は、この闇に包まれた時間を、妖怪や魑魅魍魎が活動する時間として恐れていたのです。④では、なぜ夜に爪を切ってはいけないのでしょうか。⑤爪を切るときには刃物を使います。⑥刃物には霊力が宿るなどと考えられ、また、魔よけの道具ともされていました。

⑦その一方、刃物を体に当てることで、その霊力により体に隙ができるとも考えられていたのです。⑧夜は悪霊が活発にうごめく時間帯ですから、体に隙ができれば、そこから悪霊たちが体内に入ってきてしまうと思われていたのです。

82. Hide Your Thumbs at the Sight of a Funeral Car

①People often say, "You won't be able to be with your parents when they die if you don't <u>hide</u> your <u>thumbs</u> at the
隠す　　　親指
<u>sight of</u> a <u>funeral car</u>," or "Your parents will <u>die young</u> if
～を見て　霊柩車　　　　　　　　　　　　若くして死ぬ
you don't hide your thumbs when you see a funeral car."

②Some people even hide their thumbs when they see a
<u>funeral</u> or <u>pass</u> a <u>grave</u>, <u>as well as</u>, when they see a funeral
葬式　　～を通る 墓　　～だけでなく
car. ③<u>This may be why</u> thumbs make people think of their
これは～だからかもしれない
parents because the Japanese word for thumb is *oya-yubi*,
which means "parent finger."

④The first funeral car <u>appeared</u> in Japan in the *Taisho*
現れた
period. ⑤Before that, there were <u>various</u> other <u>folk beliefs</u>
さまざまな　　　大衆の信仰(→俗信)
about thumbs. ⑥For example, people believed they wouldn't
get sick if they hid their thumbs. ⑦People thought sickness
<u>was caused by</u> <u>evil spirits</u> <u>entering</u> their bodies from <u>under</u>
～によって引き起こされた　悪い霊　～に入る
their thumbnails.
親指の爪のあいだ
⑧<u>The Japanese</u> have always thought that death is <u>unclean</u>.
日本人　　　　　　　　　　　　　　　　　　　　けがれた

⑨People also think that the spirit that has just died is
死んだばかりの霊魂
dangerous because they might catch its uncleanness.
けがれ
⑩That spirits of the dead and also evil spirits, which are
邪悪な霊
thought to bring about death, are wandering around the
〜をもたらす　　　　　　〜の周りをさまよう
funeral car. ⑪People hide their thumbs to keep them from
〜が―しないようにする
entering their body through their thumbnails.

---

82. 霊柩車を見たら、親指を隠す

①「霊柩車(れいきゅうしゃ)を見たら親指を隠さないと、親の死に目に会えない」、「親を早く亡くす」などといわれることがあります。②霊柩車だけではなく、葬式を見たときや墓の前を通るときにも親指を隠す人がいます。③これらは、親指が親を連想させるからでしょう。

④日本に霊柩車が登場するのは大正時代です。⑤それ以前から親指にまつわるさまざまな俗信がありました。⑥たとえば、「親指を隠すと疫病(えきびょう)にかからない」といったものがあります。⑦疫病は悪い霊の仕業(しわざ)であり、親指の爪のあいだから悪い霊が体内に入り込むと思われていたようです。

⑧日本人は死をけがれと考えてきました。⑨そして、死んだばかりの霊魂は、死のけがれを感染させる、大変に危険なものとされてきました。⑩死者の霊魂や死をもたらす悪霊や邪霊は、霊柩車の周りにさまよっています。⑪親指を隠すのは、それらが親指から体内に入るのを防ぐといった意味もあるのでしょう。

The Chinese zodiac / 十干十二支

....

The ten Heavenly Stems, or *jikkan*, were used to count dates in ancient China. They divided a month into three parts and named ten days in each part: Jia (甲), Yi (乙), Bing (丙), Ding (丁), Wu (戊), Ji (已), Geng (庚), Xin (辛), Ren (壬), Gui(癸).

The twelve Earthly Branches, or *juni-shi*, come from the ancient Chinese astronomy. Since the Jupiter takes 12 days to go around the earth, people can count the number of years by dividing the equator into twelve parts and seeing the Jupiter's position. People counted down these twelve parts according to the movement of the sun and gave animal names such as Rat, Ox, Tiger, Rabbit and so on. It is called the Earthly Branches. The Stems-Branches, *kan-shi*, mean the ten Heavenly Stems, the twelve Earthly Branches, or 60 combinations of them.(see the next page)

十干は、古代中国の日付の数え方でした。1ヵ月を上旬、中旬、下旬に三分し、10日ずつまとめて甲、乙、丙、丁、戊、己、庚、辛、壬、癸と呼び、日数を数えました。

十二支は、古代中国の天文学から生まれたものです。木星は約12年かけて地球を一周するため、赤道を12等分して木星の位置を見れば、年を知ることができます。これを太陽の運行にあわせて、子、丑、寅、卯……と動物の名前をつけたものが十二支です。「干支」とは、十干、十二支、あるいはこのふたつの60通りの組み合わせです(次ページ参照)。

55 戊午 (つちのえうま)	49 壬子 (みずのえね)	43 丙午 (ひのえうま)	37 庚子 (かのえね)	31 甲午 (きのえうま)	25 戊子 (つちのえね)	19 壬午 (みずのえうま)	13 丙子 (ひのえね)	7 庚午 (かのえうま)	1 甲子 (きのえね)
56 己未 (つちのとひつじ)	50 癸丑 (みずのとうし)	44 丁未 (ひのとひつじ)	38 辛丑 (かのとうし)	32 乙未 (きのとひつじ)	26 己丑 (つちのとうし)	20 癸未 (みずのとひつじ)	14 丁丑 (ひのとうし)	8 辛未 (かのとひつじ)	2 乙丑 (きのとうし)
57 庚申 (かのえさる)	51 甲寅 (きのえとら)	45 戊申 (つちのえさる)	39 壬寅 (みずのえとら)	33 丙申 (ひのえさる)	27 庚寅 (かのえとら)	21 甲申 (きのえさる)	15 戊寅 (つちのえとら)	9 壬申 (みずのえさる)	3 丙寅 (ひのえとら)
58 辛酉 (かのととり)	52 乙卯 (きのとう)	46 己酉 (つちのととり)	40 癸卯 (みずのとう)	34 丁酉 (ひのととり)	28 辛卯 (かのとう)	22 乙酉 (きのととり)	16 己卯 (つちのとう)	10 癸酉 (みずのととり)	4 丁卯 (ひのと・う)
59 壬戌 (みずのえいぬ)	53 丙辰 (ひのえたつ)	47 庚戌 (かのえいぬ)	41 甲辰 (きのえたつ)	35 戊戌 (つちのえいぬ)	29 壬辰 (みずのえたつ)	23 丙戌 (ひのえいぬ)	17 庚辰 (かのえたつ)	11 甲戌 (きのえいぬ)	5 戊辰 (つちのえたつ)
60 癸亥 (みずのとい)	54 丁巳 (ひのとみ)	48 辛亥 (かのとい)	42 乙巳 (きのとみ)	36 己亥 (つちのとい)	30 癸巳 (みずのとみ)	24 丁亥 (ひのとい)	18 辛巳 (かのとみ)	12 乙亥 (きのとい)	6 己巳 (つちのとみ)

【参考図書】

『日本人の春夏秋冬』(新谷尚紀 / 著) 小学館

『お葬式—死と慰霊の日本史』(新谷尚紀 / 著) 吉川弘文館

『先祖供養のしきたり』(新谷尚紀 / 著) ベスト新書

『なぜ日本人は賽銭を投げるのか』(新谷尚紀 / 著) 文春新書

『日本人の縁起かつぎと厄払い』(新谷尚紀 / 著) 青春出版社

『民俗学がわかる事典』(新谷尚紀 / 編著) 日本実業出版社

『なるほど！民俗学』(新谷尚紀 / 著) ＰＨＰ研究所

『都市の暮らしの民俗学』1〜3巻 (新谷尚紀・岩本通弥 / 編) 吉川弘文館

『暮らしの中の民俗学』1〜3巻 (新谷尚紀・湯川洋司・波平恵美子 / 編) 吉川弘文館

『日本のしきたりがわかる本』(新谷尚紀 / 監修) 主婦と生活社

『和のしきたり』(新谷尚紀 / 監修) 日本文芸社

『和の暮らし大事典』(新谷尚紀 / 監修) 学習研究社

『日本人なら知っておきたい暮らしの歳時記』(新谷尚紀 / 監修) 宝島社新書

『日本人の禁忌』(新谷尚紀 / 監修) 青春出版社

『日本の「行事」と「食」のしきたり』(新谷尚紀 / 監修) 青春出版社

『結婚式　幸せを創る儀式』(石井研士 / 著) 日本放送出版協会

『阿含経を読む　下巻』(三枝充悳 / 著) 青土社

『日本民俗大辞典』上・下巻　吉川弘文館

監修者

新谷尚紀（しんたに　たかのり）
1948年広島県生まれ。早稲田大学第一文学部史学科卒業、同大学院博士課程修了。現在、国立歴史民俗博物館教授、総合研究大学院大学文化科学研究科教授。民俗学者。社会学博士（慶應義塾大学）。
主な著書には、『日本人の春夏秋冬』（小学館）、『日本のしきたりがわかる本』（主婦と生活社）、『和のしきたり』（日本文芸社）、『民俗学がわかる事典』（日本実業出版社）ほか、多数ある。

Andrew P. Bourdelais（アンドリュー P. ボーダレー）
1971年米国ウィスコンシン州生まれ。在日歴、英語講師歴ともに14年以上の大ベテラン。公立中学校のリスニング試験問題や英語学習ソフトのレコーディング、翻訳経験を経て、現在は京都府にて英会話スクール『English Oasis』を経営。
「英語のまぐまぐ！」（http://english.mag2.com/qa_business/）にて「ネイティブ表現トレーニング　ビジネス編」を連載中。
主な著書には、執筆協力者として『留学しないで、英語の超★達人！』、『同僚に差をつける！毎朝10秒のビジネス英語習慣』（中経出版）ほかがある。

＊本書は書き下ろしオリジナルです。

じっぴコンパクト新書　045

伝えたい"ニッポンの心"！
英語対訳で読む日本のしきたり
Japanese Traditions in Simple English

2009年10月10日　初版第1刷発行
2015年　7月　7日　初版第5刷発行

監修者…………**新谷尚紀＋Andrew P. Bourdelais**
発行者…………**増田義和**
発行所…………**実業之日本社**
　　　　　〒104-8233　東京都中央区京橋3-7-5　京橋スクエア
　　　　　電話（編集）03-3535-2393
　　　　　　　　（販売）03-3535-4441
　　　　　http://www.j-n.co.jp/
印刷所…………**大日本印刷**
製本所…………**ブックアート**